ELLY'S HOBO REFORMATION

NR Tidd

Second Edition

...

(formerly titled: *Ray and Elly*)

Copyright © 2008

ISBN 978-0-6151-7069-5

CONTENTS

RAKE AND HOE MAKER TROUBLE 1
HAVE BIBLE WILL TRAVEL 5
SALVATION SHELTER 8
BURIED TREASURE 11
RED EYE 14
A CAPITAL AFFAIR 17
CAPITAL ENCORE 20
MAIL CALL 23
STOWAWAYS 28
FIGURE IT OUT AND RACIAL RADIO 31
SOUTHERN TROUBLE 35
CUBANS ON THE CUSP 39
HOSTILE TAKE OVER 42
HOBOES ALOFT 45
OLLIE'S REVIVAL 48
SMOKE STORY 51
SHOW TIME 54
HOLY PROFITS AND WOMEN WITH HORNS 57
STEEPLE TRANSMISSION AND METRIC TIME 60
GLANCING GLASSES AND BODY MODIFICATIONS 63
ACTIVE RECEPTION 66
BOG'S JOBS 69
AIR TEXT 72
AIR BORNE GRAFFITI AND AUDIENCE EVALUATION 75
MARITAL REVOLUTION 78
PERSONAL PROPERTY AND SPIRITUAL INCOME 81

HANDICAP HEAT	84
SIGNS OF SPEECH	87
BUS BOYS AND RADIO RELICS	90
SINGING THE BLUES	93
MOBIL MEETINGS AND AIRBORNE MESSAGES	96
THE DEFENSE REALLY RESTS	99
TAKE ME OUT OF THE BALL GAME	102
BOG'S THE BOSS	106
HIGHER AND HIRED	109
SLIPPERY SLOPES	112
DRAWN AND REFORMED	115
STANLEY STINKER	118
HIT THE LIGHTS	120
MENSA MISFITS	123
UNCOMMON SENSE	126
SHIFTY BUSINESS	129
PHONE ARCADE	132
WHO'S THAT KNOCKIN'	135
HASTY COMPOST POWER	138
GET YOUR EYES ON THE ROAD	141
NOW HE'S GONE TOO FAR	144
RING IN THE HAT	147
FRAGILE FOOTING	150
GHOSTLY GAS	153
THE MEETING WILL COME TO CHAOS	156
TAKE THIS WOMAN	159
NOT *TOO* SMART	162
SENIOR THUG	165

WAG THE BOG	168
FAST GAS	171
GLAD WAGS AND NO SELF SERVICE	174
HOLY HANDOUTS	177
HAPPY NEW YEAR YOURSELF	180
FUGITIVES ON THE LOOSE	183
NO CIGARS	186
HAULED OFF	189

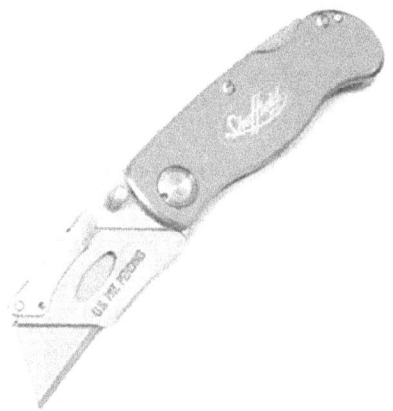

RAKE AND HOE MAKER TROUBLE

ELLY HAD TO STAB A MAN LAST NIGHT. She's sure someone will be after her, so she left her room and is hiding out a few miles south at her sister's bed and breakfast, but doesn't dare to stay there too long.

She was working after hours at Cheshire Rake and Hoe on some spreadsheets when one of the mill's lathe men, Riv Boolemon (Boolie), came in complaining that he didn't get all of the overtime pay that he had coming. She explained that, although she uses the time cards for labor distribution and analysis reports, she had nothing to do with payroll nor did they even see her data. He wasn't convinced and insisted that she should show her figures to Accounting and straighten them out. As he began reciting his entire weekly time sheet totals to her, he came closer and held her attention by grabbing her wrist with his gritty hand. He smelled like rancid olive oil.

She jerked her arm free but, with a quick and bitting grip, he reattached himself and, with his humid breath hitting her face, impatiently continued his complaint. She tried to pull away but his hand held like a clamp as he kept talking. She shouted for him to let her go and struck the back of his hand as hard as she could. He stopped talking, bit his lip and tightened his face but the clamp held steady.

He studied her for a few dreadfully long seconds, then relaxed his eyebrows and let her hand fall. He became very apologetic and gently rubbed her red arm. She pulled away and he calmly left without saying anything else. She was pretty rattled but had to get her report done for a morning meeting, so got back to work on it.

An hour or more later, Boolie came back. Drunk. Again, he grabbed her wrist and continued his earlier apology and request for overtime pay while again rubbing her arm with his other hand. She told him to leave but he only smiled and expanded his rubbing past her elbow. Since Boolie's been at the plant, she's noticed that he's had his eye on her more than once. Although well into her fifties, she was still in pretty good shape and had a strong feeling that he was considering getting something other than overtime pay. She had always been worried about a situation like this. To the point where she constantly carried a folding pocket utility knife. The main advantage is that it has a little pin for changing the blade which also lets you open it with one hand. It was in the right front pocket of her jeans but Boolie was holding that arm.

It's not easy to reach in your front pocket with the opposite hand but, with a bending twist, she did it and got the blade clicked open. He didn't notice. As calmly as she could, she told him to let her go or she'd hurt him. He laughed and kept rubbing.

There come a few points in life where you decide to execute a life changing decision. You take the pen and sign on the dreadful line; you check the box; you pull the curtain, throw the switch, slam the door. You bite the bullet. She took a deep breath, pulled the trigger and thrust her knife into her fears with a deliberate force

It was an awkward backhand blow with her left hand, but she got him squarely in the upper right chest. She thought it would be like sticking into a raw ham. Instead, the blade hit on a diagonal between two of his ribs and twisted itself straight; causing the metal handle to turn in her grip scraping her palm. It hurt, but she held on tight until the blade was fully planted.

He gasped and his eyes went wide. She pulled the knife out. He slumped and she was able to push him back. He clutched the hole and dark blood leaked out between his fingers. He shook his other gritty fist at her and screamed in a high shrill what sounded like: "By Faley, I *weel* surely *kill* you!" Then ran out the door, dripping and howling some unintelligible string of curses. Her heart never beat so hard; she stood frozen for at least a minute. It's a little blade and she was sure he'd live, but she knew stabbing someone is more than likely to get the police's attention and it will certainly lead to some frightful retaliation. She quickly e-mailed the unfinished report, wrote a short resignation for the boss, ran to her rooming house, packed what she could in one bag, left a note and a check for the landlady and lit out.

She spent the night with the knife on the dresser, worrying about how to get rid of it and wondering who the hell *Faley* was.

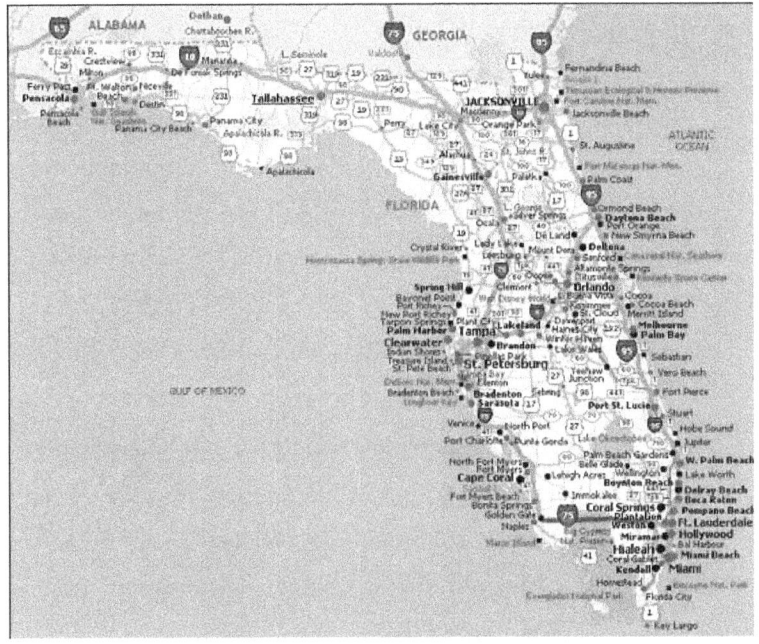

HAVE BIBLE WILL TRAVEL

ELLY'S STILL AT RUBY'S but she'll be heading south with a traveling minister. A unique fellow who's been staying at the Inn. He and Orchard, the retired lawyer next door, have become good friends. Orchard always comes over in the evenings to visit Ruby and to smoke his pipe. The minister, Ray Aker, is a cigar man, so they've been smoking together the past few nights and having a grand time. Ruby complains about the smell but Elly knows she likes the company. Elly likes to have a cigar once in a while herself (Ruby keeps a box of

Coronas for her) so she's been smoking with both of them and listening to Ray's stories. He's a contract minister who's just finished a job up the street and is on his way to another in Florida. By "contract" he means that he's a *substitute* preacher who fills in for various ministers out of the mainstream who go on vacation or otherwise need someone to fill in for them. He says he mostly keeps going directly from one job to the next up and down the East coast. Elly asked him when does he get a chance to go home. He says he has no home and only takes jobs that include lodging (this church is paying his rent). Ruby didn't think any one could make a living as a part time preacher. He says he doesn't need much now that he's old enough to get a little from Social Security. That, and without a house or car, his cost of living is pretty low. It sounded like a fairly unstable situation to Elly but he seems pretty comfortable with it.

He also seems to be in a perpetual good mood and one would get the impression that he's going to burst out laughing at any moment. He's a lanky black man with an odd characteristic of talking to strangers as though he's always known them. Elly said he looked a little like Morgan Freeman with a beard. He says Elly looks like Emmylou Harris, she was hoping he'd say "Nicole Kidman's older sister" but can't complain.

Orchard told Ray about Ruby's late husband, Ollie, and his stint as a preacher and how he helped Ollie set up the *Ollie Khan Revival Church*. It's an old Baptist church across from the Inn that they bought for next to nothing about twenty five years ago. Ollie didn't really preach, he mostly read to them or told stories and they always looked forward to it. It was more of a social club than a church, but Elly guessed a few of them are like that. Orchard says it works both ways, where a lot of clubs are set up like religions and expect the same level of loyalty.

For music, they had a piano that Elly used to play and she'd sometimes sing. Ray was impressed and said that she could be *his* organist (if an organ turned up), said it could help pick up the turn out. She knew he was kidding but jumped at the opening and asked if she could come with him to Florida. He was somewhat stunned and didn't know what to say. She told him about the fix she was in and he seemed sympathetic. He said the police have been after him before and he knows how it feels but said it wouldn't work out and confessed that he usually hitchhikes between jobs, and sleeps outdoors on the way. She told him that she loved to camp out and that she's also had to hitchhike from time to time. He was reluctant but she was enthusiastic and he finally gave in. Ruby's fit to be tied but Elly's excited and relived. They leave tomorrow.

SALVATION SHELTER

ELLY FINDS HERSELF IN HAMPTON BEACH, sitting on the front steps of a United Methodist Church. To her left is the road back to Route 1A. To her right is the ocean with a lot of small choppy white waves rolling in. A few of the shops were open, including a seafood stand where she introduced Ray to fried clams. Now, he's across the street, in front of her, in one of those red four by eight Salvation Army clothing drop-off sheds. She sees him with his head sticking out of the chute where you drop your old clothes in. He's motioning for her to come over. That's where they're sleeping tonight.

She thought back to this morning when Orchard came over and talked with Ray for quite a while on the dock. The Inn is right on the banks of the Connecticut River. For some reason, Ollie and

Orchard liked to call it *Ruby's River*. It was interesting to see them together; Ray with his grayish black hair and beard and bald Orchard with his snow white moustache, (one of those big bushy ones like Mark Twain had). Ray learned that Ruby's real name is *Elisabeth* and that "Ruby" is just a nick name that Ollie gave her years ago. They also learned that Ray's name is not short for *Raymond*; rather, it's short for *Razer*. "Probably a curse from his mother," Ruby later calculated. Ray travels with just a shoulder bag and an umbrella (a long one that he uses like a cane). Elly's bag was similar and she packed up as much as she thought she could carry, including the knife.

    Between the two of them, they've got about $1200 which Ray says should be enough to keep them going for quite a while. Once packed, Louie Wing, the Franco-Asian mechanic who lives in an old Esso station down the street, gave them a ride to the Keene bus stop in his Dodge. It's an old model with a bench seat that Louie needs for both of his girl friends to sit up front. (He only dates girls in pairs and refuses to go out with only one at a time. If the girls fight among themselves, he breaks up with both of them).

    They could have caught a bus to Hartford, but Ray felt more comfortable hitchhiking. He also wanted to see the ocean so they went over to Route 101 and started walking east with Elly in front. When a car came, they'd both turn with their thumbs out. This way, Ray would be facing the car first, with her behind. They got a couple of rides without much trouble; the last one was in a white cargo van that said:

        "Ansie's Orchid Farm
        Brattleboro Vermont"

on the side. Inside, Ansie herself was at the wheel. Elly sat up front with her while Ray rode in back with the orchids. Elly and Ansie talked a lot, and when she found out that Elly and Ray were on their way to Florida, she got all excited. It turns out that she gets most of her orchids from Florida but she's never been further south than New York City.

They delivered a few trays to a florist shop in Epping. From there, she drove to Hampton for the last delivery and then dropped them off at the beach before heading back to Vermont.

It was a pretty warm day and they spent the rest of the afternoon sitting on the sand. When you see vacation commercials, they always show people on the beach, yet here they are, like the rest of the tourists but with no expenses to be paid. Elly thinks, it's been an adventure and suspects it'll be an interesting night in the Salvation Army box; at least neither Boolie nor the police will find her there.

BURIED TREASURE

ELLY NOW FINDS HERSELF CAMPED IN A CLOVERLEAF. Specifically, they're in a small glade on a little hill in the southwest loop of the cloverleaf formed by the intersection of Routes 495 and 2, where Ray has a campsite already established. A few years ago, he cleared this spot and buried a large, watertight plastic container filled with camping supplies including tarps, ropes, a folding army shovel and an air mattress with an air pump, and finally, an old olive jar with $120 in it. He calls this one of his "Eisenhower Islands" and says he's got a few others set up along the East coast.

As Elly watches, Ray has the rope stretched between two trees and the larger tarp draped over it, making a green tent. Under the tent, he has another tarp spread out on the ground and he's busy pumping up the air mattress. Luckily it's a queen size version, so she felt it should be roomier than last night.

The Salvation Army box wasn't as nice as it sounds. A four by eight foot space sounds like a lot of room but it wasn't. Nevertheless, it was fairly comfortable but stuffy and musty, much like living in a large hamper. They slept on a mattress of recycled clothes and covered up with old coats. She didn't think of packing a blanket and couldn't help but wonder what other vagrant creatures might be wanting to move in.

It would have been a relatively nice night, but not long after they got to sleep, a small pickup carrying an unhappy couple pulled up. They heard a car door open, followed by shuffling footsteps toward them and then three trash bags full of clothes came flying in. They were light and bounced off the back wall. Then, a young man's voice hollered from the car:

"Come on Mindy, let's move it!"

"Oh hold your underwear!" replied the angry Mindy. "This would go quicker if you helped!" she snapped.

The young man grumbled something, but didn't come out. With more foot steps, they heard the girl struggling a bit and suddenly a heavy bag, full of what turned out to be old sneakers, fell through the opening and landed right on Ray. Elly quickly slapped her hand over his mouth, in case he was going to holler, but he only tried to moan.

The rest of the night was quiet and they slept well. In the daylight, she picked through the clothes to see if there was anything they could use. About all she came up with was a denim vest that would have fit Ray, but he didn't want it.

Getting out of the box was a little trickier for Elly than getting in. Ray's slept in these before and made it look easy but Elly got a splinter.

After cleaning up in the public restrooms, they left the beach and headed south. He didn't feel like hitchhiking and they walked all the way to Newburyport, which took a couple of hours. On the way, they crossed over the Merrimack River; Elly thought of throwing her knife in but didn't dare.

Once over the bridge, they were in Newburyport and went shopping downtown where Elly bought a hat; sort of a fishing hat; light green with a wide brim. They also bought a fleece blanket that was surprisingly light but they says it's as warm as wool. They spent a little time down at the docks watching the boats and wondering what it would be like to live on one. Leaving the boats, they made their way to Route 110 and resumed hitchhiking, getting a ride all the way to Chelmsford in a Buick station wagon. From there they rode in a newspaper delivery van to Littleton then walked the rest of the way to the cloverleaf.

It's a nice little spot protected by the off ramp loop, (much like an asphalt moat) and no one would ever know someone was living there. If it had running water, she'd think of settling in, even thought it was her job to dig the latrine.

RED EYE

IT'S DARK AND THEY'RE RIDING ON A BUS through New Jersey on their way to Washington, D. C. It's a long trip, so they'll be sleeping right on the bus.

In spite of the traffic whizzing around them the night before, Elly slept well. After packing up, they started walking south on 495. Ray still didn't feel like hitchhiking which made Elly worry about another long walk. She asked him if it was because of her, and without hesitating he said "Yes." Before she could protest, he explained that when he was alone, traveling was always a bit of a struggle and that most people were rather cautious with him. Getting a ride was always a high point. But, with her around, he says it's like he's no longer a threat and that he can see the difference in people's eyes. He says it's as though she had elevated him to a legitimate social status. So, although he's glad to have her with him, he says she's made hitchhiking too easy.

She was still stewing over it when they came upon a tractor-trailer stopped in a small turn-off area with its diesel engine running. As they walked past, and just as she was thinking that it's too bad that trucks aren't as easy to hop a ride on as trains are, the cab's passenger door swung open and a young woman stuck her head out, asking if they needed a lift. Elly was afraid Ray would say no. So she quickly said "Sure!" and started climbing up. Ray followed and they squeezed together in the passenger seat.

Her name was "Holly Moffit," she lived by herself and this was her own rig. She was hauling wood pellet stoves and gets paid by the mile. Ray later said that's why truck drivers often seem to be in such a hurry; the more ground they cover in a month, the more they make. She didn't seem to be in much of a hurry today and she brought them all the way to a truck stop in Connecticut where she took on fuel and headed on to New York and Pennsylvania, leaving them behind.

The truck stop was a full service complex. Ray and Elly had a late breakfast followed by coin-operated showers. The truck stop even had a laundry mat, so they washed up what little laundry they had. Once cleaned up, Elly called Ruby to let her know where they were and that everything was okay. But Black Ivy answered instead. She was watching the place while Ruby went on an errand with Orchard to Concord. Black Ivy lives across and down the street with Ollie's nephew, Bog.

She's a dark haired Cuban with sharp, Egyptian-like, soul piercing eyes. She's also a private pilot and has a small airplane and a 1,500 foot grass landing strip behind their house. She uses it to tow advertising banners wherever the crowds are. Elly asked her how Bog was doing and she said that she had to send him to the couch for a nap. It seems they got a new cable TV service and Bog found a late-night show about nude figure skating that kept him up until 4:00 and left him with a dreadful set of red eyes.

Black Ivy's an exceptionally intense woman with an occasionally fierce disposition, but she surprisingly lets Bog get away with a lot and he seems to thrive on her tolerance. With his thick curly hair and cherub-like grin, he gives the impression of being a renegade Hobbit who's just waiting for his diabolical practical joke to be discovered

Outside the truck stop laundry, Ray and Elly found a bus stop and sat there smoking cigars for a half hour until one showed up and took them to New York City where they changed to another. It was pretty comfortable and Ray was busy snoring. This was much better than hitchhiking she thought.

A CAPITAL AFFAIR

RAY AND ELLY ARRIVED IN WASHINGTON. It was raining, so they spent a few hours hanging around a Marriott Hotel lobby reading their newspapers and relaxing in large leather chairs. She was a little nervous, but with their bags they looked like normal travelers so they didn't have any trouble. They even got a free continental breakfast. Ray says that the trick to being a hobo is not to look like one (she was glad they were able to clean-up the day before).

    The rain didn't let up very much so they spent the afternoon in one of the Smithsonian museums. Once it got dark, they went to another one of his pre-packaged campsites. This one was past the Lincoln Memorial and over the bridge into Arlington. It was nowhere near as nice as the last one. It was just an area on the side of an isolated part of the road in a patch of juniper bushes. It's not on a hill either, so they were right down at the same level as the traffic, which was very unsettling for Elly.

She didn't sleep very well but they had tarps (just like before) and the new fleece blanket, so at least they stayed warm and dry. Ray said it's very important to stay dry when it's cold. But today it's warm and she's sitting in the sun against a tree on the grassy Mall (not far from the Washington Monument) and they're not alone. There are assorted beggars, musicians, and costumed and painted mimes. One of the more curious performers was a man dressed in a mesh of leaves. He was holding a couple of leafy branches and would crouch down near the sidewalk and remain perfectly still, looking entirely like a bush until someone would walk by. As they approached, he would wiggle the branches and make them jump. Many of the surprised pedestrians would make a donation to his coffee can and walk away laughing.

Amidst all this entertainment, Ray's also performing. He's standing on a bench and delivering a somewhat solemn sermon (he calls it *sidewalk preaching*). Elly thinks he's very articulate and quite interesting to listen to but he's not attracting much of a crowd. His hat is upside down on the ground in front of him and it's collected a little over $20 so far. He showed her a list of his sermons whose titles included:

Is the World Better Off With You Around?,

Are We Using Our Time Or Just Counting Events?,

Don't Get Caught Alone, (she liked this one),

Who'll Be Glad When You're Gone? (She didn't like that one)

and

Desire and Misery or How to be Happy For No Reason At All.

He preaches for about twenty minutes, then breaks for about ten before starting up again. On the last break, she told him that these titles didn't sound very religious. He said they weren't but says when he ties them in with a bit of scripture, he gets away with it. She said that at least he's a *God fearing* man. He told her not to take too much for granted. Now she doesn't know what to think.

He was hoping to raise $100 before heading south, so it looks like they'll be here again tomorrow. She thought his presentation was pretty good but also thought they needed to spice it up a bit. Noticing a bit of a cadence in his speech gave her an idea that she'll try tomorrow.

CAPITAL ENCORE

THINGS WENT PRETTY WELL the next day, and they made more money to boot. Last night, they finished up with nearly $60 which was okay but Ray was hoping to do a little better. After visiting some of the memorials, they got supper in a steamy little chili bar (not far from the capital) but she had to hurt Ray while they were there.

As the waitress was bringing their drinks, she thought she caught him staring at her chest so she made him stop right away by giving him a firm kick in the ankle. It made his jaw drop and his eyebrows pull together. After the waitress left he recovered and claimed that he was just distracted by the crucifix she was wearing around her neck. Elly didn't buy it but he went on saying how he thinks it's odd that people think of the cross as something special or holy. He says it was simply the current mechanism for executions 2,000 years ago. Then he says: "Suppose they were *hanging* people at the time, would all the Christians be wearing little golden hangman's nooses around their necks?" Elly thought he was being ridiculous and told him that was the stupidest thing she ever heard and that he deserved the kick after all.

Afterwards, she found a small music shop and poked around and bought a harmonica. He complained that she shouldn't be spending that much but she insisted and told him that they needed it to score tomorrow's performance. They also went into an office supply place where she bought two of those plastic file boxes that look like milk crates, a thick poster board and a broad felt tip marker.

Once it got dark, they went back to the campsite but they still had a little light from the street lamps so she was able to draw up a poster saying:

"Ray and Elly
Contract Ministry
Services ..."

Ray said it sounded like an enforcement agency for the Vatican.

In the morning, they got more free hotel coffee and muffins, then set up near the same spot on the Mall. She stacked up their bags in a sunny spot about ten feet from the sidewalk and leaned the poster in front of them. She placed one of the crates for him to stand on beside it and the other behind the poster, where *she* stood.

As people began walking by, he started his first sermon, but this time Elly provided background music with the harmonica. A surprising number of people stopped to listen and they had a few bills dropped into his upturned hat right away. During the breaks between sermons, she stayed on her crate and filled in with complete songs. Sometimes on the harmonica and sometimes singing tunes like *Amazing Grace, Shelter From The Storm, Love Letters From Your Heart*, and so on. She'd even sing a little during his sermons but softly and only with lyrics that tied in with his story line. During his W*ho'll Be Happy When You're Gone* speech, she quietly sang *Tom Dooley* and had a couple of people crying. Overall, the routine went really well and, by mid-afternoon, they had taken in just over $400. Elly was thrilled. As they were packing up, a few people even asked for their autographs. She told Ray she'd make him famous. He said it would be the other way around.

They stashed the poster and crates behind one of the Smithsonian maintenance sheds and went to a small Peruvian restaurant where they had a spicy supper (her tongue was still on fire). They'll hit the road tomorrow.

MAIL CALL

ELLY'S GOT MAIL. It turns out that Ray has a floating mailbox across the bridge in Alexandria. That is, his mail's sent to a private mail box company and he can have it directed anywhere. He had given the address to Ruby and Ruby gave it to Black Ivy's little girl, Carla and she sent a letter.

    They picked it up after taking the Metro there and will be sleeping in a real bed tonight. It further turns out that Ray maintains his legal residency in Alexandria and does it through this lady's rooming house. He pays her a couple hundred dollars a year and she lists him as a tenant. They were going to hit the road after Ray paid towards his rent but the lady insisted that they stay for the night. Ray later told Elly that this was the first time he's stayed over. It's a pleasant little room on the third floor with sloping ceilings and a view of the river. She told him that he should find more campsites like this one.

CARLA'S LETTER

HELLO MIZZ ELEANOR -
I HOPE YOU ARE O K. LADY KHAN SAYS YOU AND A FRIEND ARE ON A ADVENTURE. I HOPE YOUR ADVENTURE IS EXCITING.
MOM SAYS SHE HOPES YOUR SAFE. ME TO.
IM HAVING A GOOD TIME. UNCLE BOG WATCHES ME WHILE MOM WORKS ON THE WEEKEND FLYING SIGNS OVER THE BEACHES. SOMETIMES WE FISH AND SOMETIMES MY JOB IS TO PUSH THE HAMMOCK WHILE HE IS IN IT. OTHER TIMES HE HELPS ME WITH MY SCHOOL HOMEWORK.
LIKE THE TIME MY TEACHER MIZZ WRILL TOLD US TO COME UP WITH IDEAS TO MAKE SCHOOL MORE

FAIR.

I TOLD UNCLE BOG AND HE SAID THAT WE SHOULD REARRANGE THE ALPHABET ONCE IN A WHILE SO THAT KIDS WITH NAMES LIKE WILSON AND YOUNG WOULDNT ALWAYS HAVE TO HAVE TO STAND AT THE END OF THE LINE OR SIT IN THE BACK OF THE CLASSROOM. HE SAID I SHOULD BE THE ONE TO HAVE THE IDEA SINCE IM ONE OF THE LUCKY KIDS WHOS NAME STARTS WITH A.

SO I WROTE UP A PLAN WHERE WE WOULD MIX UP 26 BLOCKS WITH LETTERS ON THEM IN A BASKET AND PICK THEM OUT ONE AT A TIME LIKE THEY DO AT LADY KHANS GRANGE BINGO AND PRINT UP THE NEW LIST. WE WOULD DO THAT EVERY 2 WEEKS SO THAT EVERY ONE WOULD GET A CHANCE TO WIN ONCE EVERY YEAR.

I THOUGHT IT WOULD BE A GOOD IDEA AND THAT I WOULD GET A A+. BUT MIZZ WRILL JUST GRUNTED AND GAVE ME A REGULAR C.

IM NOT SURE BUT SOME TIMES I THINK UNCLE BOG TRIES TO GET ME IN TROUBLE. LIKE THE TIME LAST YEAR WHEN I WAS CRABBING ABOUT THE FOOD AT SCHOOL AND HE SAID I SHOULD ASK THE

CAFETERIA LADY IF SHE COULD MAKE GOFER GIZZARDS FOR LUNCH ONCE IN A WHILE.

I NEVER HEARD OF THEM BUT I ASKED HER ANYWAY AND SHE GOT REAL MAD AND TOLD MIZZ WRILL AND MIZZ WRILL MADE ME SIT INSIDE DURING RECESS THAT DAY.

I STILL DONT KNOW WHAT GIZZARDS ARE AND I DECIDED NOT TO TALK ABOUT THEM ANY MORE.

LATER, AFTER I TOLD HIM ABOUT THE TROUBLE HE CAUSED, HE SAID SOME PEOPLE ARE CONFLICTED ABOUT GIZZARDS AND MAYBE I SHOULD HAVE ASKED FOR GRISTLE BISCUITS OR CHICKADEES ON A STICK INSTEAD.

NOW I KNOW BETTER.

LADY KHAN SAYS I SHOULDNT LISTEN TO UNCLE BOG TO MUCH.

UNCLE BOG SAYS IM LUCKY TO BE SO SMART AND THAT NOT MANY KIDS GET TO KNOW SO MUCH AS ME BUT HE SAYS I SHOULD BE CAREFUL BE CAUSE ALL THIS KNOWLEDGE CAN BE DANGEROUS.

I THINK HES DANGEROUS.

ANYWAY IM TRYING TO BE CAREFUL BUT I WORRY A LOT.

I HOPE YOU AND YOUR FRIEND ARE BEING CAREFUL.
AND I HOPE YOU DONT HAVE TO WORRY TO MUCH.
YOURS TRULY,
CARLA ARCHEZ

STOWAWAYS

E LLY FINDS HERSELF ON THE ROAD AGAIN, almost literally. Specifically, they're on the Route 95 median strip just a little south of Fayetteville North Carolina in a grove of some odd little trees that she's never seen before. It's another one of his *Eisenhower Islands* with the usual tub of supplies and spare money jar but here he's got a hammock. Right now, he's laid out in it and just watching the traffic. Although this isn't a cloverleaf, it feels like an island because it's a twenty foot or so high strip of land with rock ledges going straight down on both the east and west sides and grassy slopes going gently down on the north and south ends. They can see the roofs of the cars and trucks going by. But the best part was getting there.

They rode most of the way in the front seat of a brand new, full-sized Ford sedan which was sitting in the bottom row of a car carrier. After they left the bed and breakfast this morning, they walked to a truck stop where, like last time, they had a small laundromat so they were able to do the washing. Outside, they walked around the trucks. Elly looked for Holly Moffit and her load of stoves, instead, they saw an array of trucks and trailers including sturdy Freightliners, dowdy Internationals, boxy Western Stars, stately Peterbilts and stoic looking Autocars. On the outer edge of the lot was this drab and orange Kenworth attached to a car carrying trailer that was half loaded with plain looking Ford sedans. Just for the heck of it and while no one was looking, She reached past the trailer's framework and tried the door (the back door), of one of the lower cars and it opened! With a gasp, she quickly and quietly closed it.

Her first thought was that this would be a great way to hop a ride. Ray wasn't as optimistic, he said they'd probably get arrested and anyway, they couldn't tell if it would be heading north or south. They thought about it for awhile and since it was new cars, was probably heading south. They decided to chance it. They got the laundry and slipped through the thin door opening into the back seat of the rear most car and laid still for about a half hour. Finally, they heard the cab's door open and close and the diesel engine start. Once they were moving, they rolled into the front seat and settled in. Luckily, the Kenworth turned south. In North Carolina while stopped at a toll booth, they quickly hopped out of the car and off the trailer (with no one apparently noticing) and walked the last few miles to the campsite. On the way, they passed through a residential area of several simple houses and at one place they had an odd little display, along the lines of an old bathtub buried halfway into the ground on end so that the top half forms a shrine for a statue. But this was a three foot white porcelain fixture on end with straight sides and a little curve at the top with some sort of statue propped inside it. Ray saw it and stopped walking. He seemed to be hypnotized, she had to shove him to get him moving again. He looked at her as though he were stuck in a puzzle. He told her that the shrine was a *urinal*, an upside down, old fashion urinal. She supposed it was a little odd but didn't know why he seemed so concerned by it.

FIGURE IT OUT AND RACIAL RADIO

AT THE CAMPSITE, Ray was working on a new sermon. Regretfully, Elly asked him what it was about. He said he's been studying people's passion to figure things out. He says it shows up on the surface where most of us can't resist puzzles, murder mysteries and all the 'question and answer' game shows, but it goes deeper, such that we often become obsessed by events or people we don't understand to the extent that we're repeatedly saying things like:

"I don't get it."

"What's he up to?"

"What's the scoop?"

"It doesn't add up."

"It doesn't make sense."

"What's the meaning of this?"

And when we've solved the puzzle or unraveled the mystery, we're proud to announce it to anyone who'll listen:

"Now I get it."

"I've got his number."

"So I see."

"It makes perfect sense."

"I told you so."

"Just as I thought."

"It figures."

"It's logical."

Then we're anxious for others to reach the same conclusion:

"Don't you get it?"

"Get the picture?"

"Don't you see what he's up to?"

"Wake up and smell the coffee!"

And, if someone even seems to challenges *our* cognitive skills, we're quick to respond:

"I wasn't born yesterday!"

"I didn't just fall off the turnip truck!"

"Don't you think I don't know it!"

"I forgot more than you'll ever know about ..."

So she asked him what the point of the sermon will be. He said he didn't know yet; says he's still trying to figure out what it all means. Well she certainly didn't get it and was sorry she asked.

Meanwhile, they were actually on the radio earlier that day. They got a bus to Florence, South Carolina where Ray's half brother, Ralph, lives. He's a local disc jockey and they went to the little station where Ray knew he'd be broadcasting. The girl at the reception desk knew Ray and let them in. They went to a hallway window looking into the small studio room where Ralph was on the air. He saw them and lit right up. He immediately motioned for them to come in and to keep quiet. They waited a few seconds for Ralph to read a commercial then he introduced them:

"Hey Hey it's Thunder Ray and ..." He looked at her with his eyebrows raised high.

"Eleanor Weston" she blurted out.

"Thunder Ray and Lady Eleanor!" relayed Ralph, "Right here on the *Roscoe Reddy Rock and Rumble Radio Show!*". ("Roscoe Reddy" is his stage name.) He queued up a song and while it was playing he set them up with earphones and a shared microphone. It turns out that *Thunder Ray* was Ray's racing name from years ago when he drove stock cars down here on the oval tracks.

Once they were on the air, Ralph got an overall update from Ray but he spent quite a bit of time interviewing *Lady Eleanor*. She was dreadfully nervous and being very careful not to swear. Ray, however, was very relaxed; she suspects that he's done this before. While more songs and more commercials played, he and Ralph talked about the radio business quite a bit. Ralph wants Ray to try a Radio Preaching show, says the South's silly with them.

After the visit, he gave them the key to his condo, so they get to sleep indoors again. They've also got the place to themselves until Ralph gets home from his second job at a night club called the *Last Gasp*. The funny thing for Elly was that Ralph was white. Or at least, he looked white. She couldn't figure it out so she asked Ray how that could be, or was one of them half black? He said no, but explained that Ralph is actually his *double* half brother. That is, he (Ray) had a different father and Ralph had a different mother. Well, it still doesn't make sense, and she thinks she'll be better off to forget about it.

SOUTHERN TROUBLE

BAD NEWS. Boolie's after Elly and he knows where she'll be. Ray checked his voice mail from Ralph's condo and found that Ruby left a message saying that Boolie came to the Inn last Sunday while she, Black Ivy, Orchard and Carla were out on a walk for a diabetes charity drive. Bog stayed behind and watched the place (since he has bad feet with fallen arches and pronation and can't walk more than a mile or two at a time). When Boolie showed up smiling and asking for Elly, Bog assumed he was a friend and gladly told him where she and Ray were headed and when they planned to get there. Ruby said she gave Bog hell for it and that he'd know better next time. But, the damage's done. Elly thought Ray would be upset, but, although he wasn't happy about it, he accepted the situation and seemed to be determined to deal with the problem. Being a preacher and all, she thought he would say that they should reason with Boolie or appeal to his sense of decency or something like that. Instead, he said that they'd have to get better weapons. Now, she doesn't know what to think and she's wondering what kind of weapons he has in mind.

Ruby had more bad news; some trouble about property taxes taking a big jump that she won't be able to afford. It'll be a big problem for Bog and Black Ivy too. Actually the problem's been brewing for a few months now and Orchard's been looking in to it. Meanwhile, Ruby didn't miss her chance to complain about Bog. He tends to make her mad like this fairly often and likes to make it worse, once he gets her started. This time he got her going by complaining about the diabetes charity and saying someone should have a podiatry charity for people like him. Of course that got her stirred up, but he continued, saying he'd start his own agency and call it the *Faulty Flat Foot Foundation* (the *4Fs*). He said he'd stand outside the IGA with crutches while holding a big empty coffee can and wearing a sad face. She said she chased him home after that. Perhaps he was just changing the subject; Elly was sure he feels bad.

She's feeling a little bad herself and she's also pretty tired. Ralph came in long after they went to bed. Then, a while later, both he and Ray fell into a pattern of synchronized snoring and she couldn't get any sleep. They got up early and she was able to clean the place up a bit while Ralph slept.

They left quietly and got breakfast downtown. Walking through town, they passed a house with a For Sale sign as an angry woman came stomping out the front door shouting:

"There's no way we're buying this place!" No way!"
A man following her was pleading, "But they'll clean it up. You'll never know it was there!"

The woman turned and shouted: "I'll <u>always</u> know there was a <u>dead cat</u> laying on the kitchen floor! So forget it!" Another woman, with a desperate face came out. The first woman threw herself into a cringing Volvo and slammed the door. The exasperated man followed and drove the angry woman away, leaving the realtor behind. Ray later said he had a chance to be a realtor back in the seventies but gave up the idea. Said he didn't like the industry's practice of showing the realtor's picture along with that of the house they were selling. Didn't understand the point.

Not only that, it seems like most of the houses sold end up owning and consuming the poor people caught holding the deed.

Not far from the dead cat, they came up to a house with an angry, untied dog guarding the yard. The moderately large brown dog with exposed teeth and a raised tail leaped to the sidewalk suggesting that they return the way they came. Elly's back began to sweat and she thought about her knife. Ray slowly raised his umbrella cane and pointed it at the loud dog. As he tried to bite the umbrella's tip, Ray calmly snapped it open, dramatically changing the dog's tone. Using the opened umbrella like a shield, they slowly walked around the beast with unexpected ease as he seemed to forget about Ray and Elly and was now wondering what to do with this new black round opponent. Ray says this used to happen all the time and almost anything bigger than a hat will do the trick.

They eventually found their way to a bus station and boarded a crowded, southbound Kraph's Coach. Elly watched the Georgia peanut farms roll by as thoughts of dead cats and barking dogs kept her from sleeping.

CUBANS ON THE C.U.S.P.

THEY MADE IT TO THE SUNSHINE STATE. They only got about two hours of sleep on last night's bus through Georgia, so they're both dragging. Ray doesn't have any campsites set up this far south and, because of so many homeless folks around here, it's hard to find anything. There's only a few suitable shelters and they're mostly occupied. The best they could find was a construction site where several large pieces of equipment were laying around. They hoped they could sleep under a truck or something like that. They did a little better, but not much; on the edge of the lot near a huge gravel pile, was a long flat bed trailer, the kind they use to carry bulldozers and such, with another identical flat bed trailer setting on top of it. So they're camped on top of the bottom one and under the top one which makes them something of a hobo sandwich. Anyway, it gives them a bit of a roof which is a good thing because a shower blew through a little while ago and it was pouring buckets. A little bit of the rain leaked through but they mostly kept dry. Just before the rain started, they saw a homeless family scampering between the trucks. The mother appeared to be carrying a heavy pinata and one of the kids, perhaps four or five, had a curled up banner on a pole and was trying to hit the pinata but instead was hitting the mother in the arms and back as she tried to protect it. They couldn't tell where they went. Elly was going to ask Ray what that was about but he seemed to be lost in thought himself. Later on he said that he's worried about Florida's future, with so many new poor people running around. He thinks things will get worse because, with Castro out of the picture, the United States will probably normalize relations with Cuba before long; then, there'll be a new flood of immigrants pouring in. Elly wondered how Black Ivy would feel about that.

It also reminded her of Bog's tirade last year about the illegal immigrants and other border problems in the Southwest. He says that they could solve much of the trouble moving the border further south where it's not so close nor as wide. He says we could buy the northern half of Mexico from the Mexicans (at least ten of their northern states) then we'd eventually get the rest of the Mexican States (they'd join of their own free will for the benefits), then we' only have to deal with Guatemala and Belize.

Ruby became furious and asked him how we'd pay for it.

"Canada's rich, we could get the money from them," he says.

"Why would Canada give us any money!" she hollers.

"Easy!" he says. "We'll sell Michigan to them. They'll jump at the chance!" This got Ruby's bun in a twist. So, to keep her going, he says, "Don't worry, we'll get it back in the merger."

"What merger!" she cries.

He says it's only a matter of time before we merge with Canada and create one big North American country. The only trouble, he says, will be picking out a new name. "Perhaps we can call it the 'Canadian United States and Provinces' and of course we'll all have to learn to speak French and Spanish and convert to the metric system."

Ruby was talking to herself for over a week after that, and she still gets mad if anybody brings it up. Elly can't imagine what the flag would look like. How many stars would it have?

HOSTILE TAKE OVER

TODAY THEY REACHED A TURNING POINT that will lead them home. They made it to Eau Gallie all right; they rode down the coast on a tourist bus and met up with Rick Thissel, the minister that was going to hire Ray, but the deal fell through and it's a tricky story. In spite of that, Elly can't stop thinking about last night's cherry picker battle.

After the previous night, they were really tired and were already sleeping when one of those long, fifteen passenger vans pulled into the site and nine laughing men wearing dark hats fell out of it. The moon was bright and they could see them fairly well as they wobbled their way to a pair of bucket trucks with those moveable baskets on the back like the phone companies use. These men started the two trucks and positioned them back to back and about twenty feet from each other. They put down the stabilizers and then two of the men got into the buckets (one in each) and up they went. They each had a long spongy pole in their right hand and were running the basket controls with their left. The men on the ground were cheering them on as they began to maneuver the baskets back and forth and swing the tubes like swords at each other. The object seemed to be to knock each other's hat off. At least there was a lot of swinging at each other's heads. It was a very eerie image, like dinosaur skeletons fighting in slow motion. This moonlight jousting went on for about fifteen minutes when one of the buckets jammed, leaving the man stranded in mid air. After a lot of laughing, the man in the working basket moved his machine over and picked up the disabled warrior. On the way down, the man that was picked up, reached over and knocked off his rescuer's hat. Ray says there's all kinds of odd things going on where people aren't looking.

Meanwhile, Thissel is putting them up for the night but nobody's happy. His Church, The *Eau Gallie God of Hope*, is going out of business. It seems that a rival church called the *Sea Side Saints* has set up shop just down the street in an empty grocery store. They've got a fiery young preacher, an eight piece band and plenty of seating room. One by one, the *Eau Gallie God* parishioners began migrating to the *Saints*, along with their donations. Eventually, the last few holdouts left, leaving Thissel with empty pews and an empty bank account. Thissel's sister was there and doesn't go along with any of this. She thinks he's getting what he deserves.

His mortgage on the church building was already overdue (attendance had been declining for a while) and he has no way of raising the dough. He's fairly bitter about it and figures the bank will soon auction it off.

Elly was sorry things didn't work out for Ray but she'll be glad to get out of there. Nevertheless, Ray's in good spirits and says that he's been feeling a little road weary anyway and perhaps it's time for something different. He also doesn't seem to have much sympathy for Ricky. In fact, he thinks it's pretty funny. Imagine if the Quakers ran out of money and the Congregationalists bought up all their property. He says, it could trigger a whole series of theological takeovers because the other churches would have to begin merger negotiations to strengthen their position and protect their assets; eventually, Wall Street would get involved. Ruby would say, if the Mormons merge with the Jehovah Witnesses and combine their sales forces, she'd be buying stock.

HOBOES ALOFT

THEY'RE TAKING OFF FROM MELBOURNE and on their way to Manchester. Ray says it's time for a change and that this would be a more civilized way to travel. She thinks he's growing tired of the hobo life; either that, or he's growing tired of her. They bought the tickets at a really good price; it would have cost them more to go by bus. But even better, they over-booked and asked for volunteers to get bumped. So they volunteered, got bumped, waited just a couple of hours for the next plane. For this, they gave them vouchers for a pair of free round trip tickets to anywhere in the contiguous States. They also got a free breakfast, which was good because this is one of those "no frills" flights and they didn't have anything to eat this morning at Ricky Thissel's. He offered them some Slim Jims and some grocery store doughnuts. They said no thanks and that they wanted to get going. They didn't want to tell him where they were going. Instead, they told him to tell anyone that came by looking for them, that they've gone to Key Largo.

They're not worried about Ricky. It turns out the minister's a member of a motorcycle gang. He showed them his bike, an old Vincent  Black Shadow. He was very proud of it. He was also proud of his club jacket and made Ray try it on. It was a typical motorcycle jacket with lots of zippers. Ray looked like he was ready for Marlon Brando's *Wild Ones*.

On the back, where she expected to see a *Hells Angels* logo, it had an embroidered oval insignia that read *"Sons of Perdition."* Ricky called his secular sister, who came over and gave them a ride to the Melbourne Airport in an old silver Citroen which had a back seat filled with empty candy bar wrappers. She offered each of them a Snickers as she dropped them off. They said no thanks and waved goodbye. She drove off, eating the Snickers.

The flight's going well. They changed planes and are on the last leg of the trip. It's been a clear day so they've had a nice view of the coast from time to time. Elly thought they'd see a lot of other planes in the air with them, but she hasn't seen any. A uniformed girl gave them ginger ale and a package of orange crackers with gooey cheese.

They can see Manhattan. She wishes they had spent some time there on their way down. Perhaps she can get him to go back for a visit. They could do their preaching routine in Greenwich Village like a couple of old beatniks.

They're on the approach for Manchester and there must be a strong crosswind because they're *crabbing* to the left quite a bit - that's what Black Ivy calls it. It's where you steer into the wind and fly a little sideways. Black Ivy says you just have to snap it straight just before you touch down. It's no big deal she says, as long as it's not gusting too much. Elly remembers that she says people worry too much about the landing. Although they can sometimes be tricky, she says landings are reasonably safe, while it's the *take off* that's much riskier; you're at your heaviest and the engine's straining the most it has to, and there's little or no chance to make any corrections or adjustments if things go wrong.

Ray's getting nervous.

They made it to the ground all right and riding on a bus to Keene, where Black Ivy will pick them up. The wind is still strong and Elly can feel it rocing the bus. The landing was a little rough but they made it okay, although someone in the seat behind them threw up and stunk up the place. It made her think of Thissel's Slim Jims, causing her to gag a bit. Ray was okay.

OLLIE'S REVIVAL

THEY'VE BEEN BACK FOR A WEEK and Elly's happy because Ray's staying.
She was afraid that he would just drop her off and hit the road, but Orchard has a project that will keep him busy there for quite a while.

Things were in a bit of disarray when they arrived. That wind they had in Manchester was pretty strong there too. So strong that it blew the steeple off the Ollie Khan church; it landed upside down in the little cemetery beside it. The top collapsed but it gave the image of being stuck in the ground. Bog and Louie nailed a plastic swimming pool upside down over the hole, so now it looks like the church is wearing a short blue derby hat. It's keeping the rain out so far, but Ruby says it's sacrilegious. Ray thinks it's cool, but he's not sure about the symbolic implications.

Nevertheless, Ruby was very glad to see them and made Elly promise not to run off like that again. So she'll be staying at the Inn and helping out with the housekeeping. Meanwhile, Orchard was glad to see Ray and got a similar promise out of him. Recalling that there was some trouble with the taxes, it turns out that, because they've got these seemingly wonderful waterfront locations (on the Connecticut River), Ruby, Orchard, and Bog and Black Ivy's houses have been reassessed to the point where their property taxes are going sky high. Orchard can handle it but the others can't. Although they could sell and get plenty of money for cheaper places elsewhere, nobody wants to. So, Orchard has worked out a scheme where they will all donate their property to the *Ollie Khan Church* then continue to live there as church tenants. Since none of them ever want to leave, it works out okay. Elly's the only one that Ruby would leave the Inn to, but she doesn't want it; Orchard has two sons, but they've disowned him, so he won't be leaving them anything; Bog and Black Ivy won't be able to leave their house to Carla, but Orchard's working it out so that she and her descendants will be able to live there as long as they want. At least as long as the Church is operational; which is where Ray comes in.

To make this scheme work, the church has to be a legitimate operation and having a resident minister helps a lot. Ray will have to live in the area and Ruby offered him a room at the Inn but he wasn't comfortable with the idea. Instead, he's moving into an old Winnebago-type motor home that Louie has. It doesn't run but the plumbing and propane heater work okay so, although it doesn't move, it's livable. Louie towed it behind the church and Bog and Ray have been busy getting it hooked up to the church's water and electricity. Orchard says it's illegal but suspects they'll be able to get away with it for at least a few months. It'll also help if they can keep it hidden and camouflage it. They also have to get the water and electricity turned back on for the church. Once they're able to get that worked out, services will start fairly soon, but not on Sunday. Because Ruby's usually tending guests at the Inn on weekends, while Bog and Black Ivy are towing banners, Sunday's are out. Instead, everyone agreed on Monday evenings. This will also give Ray a chance to pick up some new preaching jobs in the area; if he wants. He'll also need a new steeple.

SMOKE STORY

IT'S BEEN A BUSY WEEK but they're ready for Monday Night Church. Ruby and Elly cleaned out the chapel and washed the windows. Bog cleaned up the yard, including the cemetery and hauled off the remains of the old broken steeple. Ray and Louie took down the blue swimming pool and patched up the steeple hole with plywood and shingles. Louie and Orchard drove over to Manchester in Orchard's

Lawyer truck (an antique green International Harvester that says "O. Moss - Attorney" in gold letters followed by his five digit phone number on the doors) and bought forty eight folding chairs. Not that they expect to fill the place, but Orchard wants to be prepared just in case the notices that they tacked up all over the area stir up any interest. Black Ivy also spent the weekend flying a banner around a ten mile radius that read:

"RAY AKER @ OK CHURCH - MONDAY - 7:00."

Ray's not happy about that but they need to get a respectable audience. He also wants Elly to score the sermon like she did on the Mall in Washington. This time she'll have the piano but she also bought a neck-mounted harmonica-rack so she can play that as well. They rehearsed the presentation this afternoon and he's trying a different routine. Instead of a pat sermon, he's going to use current events and talk about what they might mean. He went through the newspaper and picked out this story about a young local couple who got arrested for robbing a grocery store in the middle of the night last week. They broke through the glass window with the front of their Jeep Wagoneer. As alarms rang, they ran in and began hauling out cartons and cartons of cigarettes and throwing them into the back of the Jeep. That's all they were after. The police arrived and blocked off the exit. The young couple took off and tried to smash their way past the police cruiser, hitting it in the side, but only managed to bust up their own front end. It turns out that they could have gotten away after all because they had the cigarettes loaded before the police arrived, but the girl was desperate for a smoke and they spent an extra few minutes trying to find a lighter in the dark checkout lanes.

When they hauled her and her boyfriend away, she was furious and demanding that the police to let her have a cigarette. So, Elly figured this was going to be a sermon about the evils of tobacco, and knowing that he loves cigars, she wondered how this was going to work. But it wasn't about tobacco.

Rather, it was about the *Dangers of Desire*. He says the element of addiction only amplifies the condition and makes the misery more acute, but this form of disappoint affects most all of us. Much of our misery, he explains, is caused by our (or someone else's) desire to get or do something. He says that it's an old philosophic notion that happiness is found not in the satisfaction of our wants, but, rather, from the absence of desire. Well, Elly's not sure it'd work if everyone felt that way. Life would sure be boring if nobody wanted anything. She worries that she'll have to make the music more cheery.

Bog listened to the rehearsal and seemed to like it. Remembering how he torments Ruby, Elly found that she's not immune. Seeing her with the harmonica neck rack reminded him that she was a big Dylan fan, so he says: "I heard Dylan's got a new CD." Elly was suckered in: "Really!" she said. "What's the Title?"

"*Dylan Sings Christmas Favorites From The Sixties*, the late night info-mercials should start any day now!" He ran off laughing before she could hit him.

SHOW TIME

ANOTHER BUSY WEEK. Elly's bohemian buddy has heat and running water in his camper. He and Bog finished hooking everything up to the church's utilities. Men also came and got the church powered up and the water running. Further, the church is a legal entity, with Elly, Ray, Orchard, Ruby, Bog, Black Ivy and Louie listed as members. Monday night services went very well. About a dozen people showed up which isn't much but they were glad anyone came. Orchard bought one of those new DVD Camcorders with a tripod and taped (or disked) the whole service. He wants to produce evidence that the church is legitimate.

Being recorded didn't bother Ray but it made Elly notice that he looked a little shabby. Not real bad, but she thinks they should both dress up a bit better next time. She played the background music while

Ray preached and she sang two solo numbers that went over pretty well.

To provide a little income and to cover expenses, they had a sign at the door saying: "$10 Donation Per Family Appreciated." Next to the sign, they had one of Ruby's glass beer brewing jugs which collected $70. On top of that, Bog collected $1.73. The fool had made a little fountain in front of the church out of the leftover kid's swimming pool. He's got a ceramic statue of a woman standing in it and had her holding a hose from an old fish tank filter pump spitting out a stream of water. He also dressed it up with assorted rocks and bark mulch so that it actually looked fairly decent. He says people will inexplicably throw money into almost any decorative pool they come across. He says you could dress up a puddle and people will throw coins in. Sure enough, several of the people going by threw something in, especially the kids.

There were more kids than they expected, so Ray came up with a children's story to open up the services. It was about the *Polliwog Princess* that lived near a Louisiana bayou. Every day she would go down to the swamp and pick out one of the frogs to kiss, to see if she could find a prince. The first frog she kissed turned into a Tel-evangelist and left to start a TV show with pious puppets in South Carolina. The next day, she kissed a second frog who turned into a cowboy that ran off to Nebraska to be a wild west politician, the third turned into a rock-n-roller with long curly purple hair who pranced off into the woods singing loud and scaring the squirrels. Ray made a hit with the kids and had some of the adults cracking up. It went on like this for a few more faulty frogs until, one day, she kissed a lonely looking fellow that didn't turn into anything at all, but was just happy to get a kiss. The princess took him home and they lived happily for many years.

Although they liked the frog story, Elly's not sure if they liked his *Dangers of Desire* sermon about the Cigarette Girlhttp://www.google.com/webhp?sourceid=navclient&ie=UTF-8. After the main sermon and one of her songs, Ray opened it up for a question and answer session. That caught the crowd off guard and it was quiet for a few long moments until Bog got things started by asking if the $10 donations were tax deductible. That drew a few groans and a punch from Ruby, but it loosened things up and others followed with a few more questions; mostly about the cigarette girl. Elly thinks she's got a few questions about that Polliwog Princess.

HOLY PROFITS AND WOMEN WITH HORNS

RAY IS SETTLING INTO HIS CAMPER; it seems to be working out okay but Elly's worried about the propane setup they've patched together. He's cleaned it up quite a bit and has also transplanted a few small pine trees around it so that it's not so noticeable.

Meanwhile, last Monday night's church session went well (Bog's been calling themselves the "*Seven Second* Day Adventists"). The crowd nearly doubled from last week; they must have told their friends; that, and Louie brought both of his girlfriends. The donation jug collected $130. On top of that, Orchard brought in $35 by selling seven DVDs of last week's 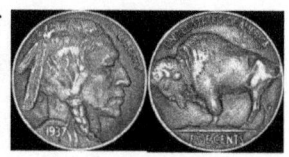 service. Bog's pretty excited too, someone tossed a buffalo nickle into his pool. Ray and Elly looked better also. She bought a light green pants suit with a soft yellow pleated blouse. She was going to dress Ray all in white but he thought that would be a little over the top. Instead, she got him a pair of black wing tipped shoes, charcoal gray dress slacks, a sharp peach colored shirt and an iridescent white tie. She thought he looked great.

Like last time, Ray started the service with a short story for the kids. This one was about a three-legged rabbit that always felt unlucky but eventually discovered that he had a lot left to be thankful for. Then, taking his queue from the news for the main sermon, he talked about the war on terror. He said that we had to brace ourselves for a long conflict and some escalation because this is actually religious war, and history shows that they're typically very prolonged and difficult to finish. Elly didn't listen too much. It was very depressing and she's worried that he'll hurt attendance if he keeps this up.

The question and answer session got a little out of hand. A self proclaimed "Born-Again Christian" (from the belligerent wing of the party) showed up and took the opportunity to give a short sermon of his own, in the form of a question. Ray was patient and let him speak but didn't respond. Bog tried to improve the mood by asking if you can get "born-again" *twice* (in case you need absolution more than once). Ray later said he'll have to start taking written questions instead. It's too bad, that was starting to be Elly's favorite part of the night.

Also among the parishioners, was an exceptionally weird couple. The boy was tattooed all over, even on his shaven head and he had what looked like miniature Christmas ornaments hanging from his ears. The girl had double pierced eyebrows and heavy black eye shadow (over and under), but mainly, her head was shaved with crisscrossed inch and a half wide strips leaving six patches or isolated pony tails of hair (three on each side). These cones (or tassels) were about eight inches long and heavily gelled so that they formed what looked like an array of horns, curling downward and pointing forward. The next day, Black Ivy and Elly were talking about the head of horns and other odd hair styles they've recently seen. Bog was there, and out of the blue, says it's a good thing women don't have beards. If they did, he says the styling variations would be overwhelming with salons on every corner producing an endless variety of facial fashions that would braid, curl and twirl women's faces in all sorts of directions. Pretty soon we'd be seeing women running around with curlers on their face. The women threw him out but Elly secretly thought she could go for a long, skinny moustache and pointy sideburns.

STEEPLE TRANSMISSION AND METRIC TIME

RAY'S HOT WATER HEATER BROKE DOWN. He's been going over to the Inn to get cleaned up as Ruby and Elly continue to try to talk him into moving there. But, instead, he's busy converting Ollie's old office (in the church attic) to a broadcast studio. It seems they're hitting the airwaves. He's been on the phone with Roscoe Ralph, who's talked him into setting up a radio station. It turns out that the FCC will grant Low Power Licenses (which are good for just a few miles) to non-profit operations, and the *Ollie Khan Church* is a perfect candidate. Ralph helped him select the transmitter and basic broadcasting equipment. It took all of his remaining money and then some. The antenna arrived yesterday and they've already installed it on the church's empty steeple platform. It's made of black angle iron and is shaped just like an elongated pyramid (four sides coming to a point). Elly thinks it looks like a burnt skeleton of the old steeple. Orchard's thrilled with the idea and is helping with the license application. Ray's also getting a machine to play CDs and tapes and he wants Elly to build a musical library, including some Classical, Bluegrass, Blues and old Rock. He's going to broadcast week nights (except Mondays of course). He's planning on a half hour story, then an hour or so of music, followed by a bedtime story for the kids. The license allows no commercials but they can advertise themselves. Bog wants to have an amateur news hour. Things like this get his mind spinning.

    Remembering his notion that The United States would merge with Canada and have to convert to the metric system, Elly learned that it gets worse. He was at the Inn for his afternoon beer when Ruby was having a difficult time adjusting the digital clock at the front desk. She would be in the fast mode and overshoot the time, then have to hold the button and wait for it to go around again. She was cursing the thing and saying she rather have an ordinary clock with hands.

    Bog perks up and says, "It'll be a lot easier when we make the switch to metric time."

    "What!" snaps Ruby.

    "I haven't heard about this and I'm not changing to any damn metric system! And why would it be any easier!?"

    "There'll only be ten hours a day, but they won't be called hours," Bog was calm and seemed serious; Elly almost believed him. "They'll be called *Decijours*, *Didges* for short."

    "What! And how many minutes in a Decijour!?"

    "One hundred. But they're not called *minutes*."

    "*Mili-minutes* I suppose!" She was turning red.

    "Almost. *Milijours*, *Midges* for short. And of course for seconds we'll have *Nanojours*, a hundred Nanojours per Milijour"

"And when's this suppose to happen!?"

"It'll be a while; they have to figure out how to handle the calendar change first."

"What calendar change!?"

"The *Metric* Calendar. Of course there will only be *ten* months, but they won't be called months ..." She chased him out before he could go any further.

Otherwise, things seem to be stabilizing for Elly. Although she still worries about Boolie, everyone else is aware of it and they'll be ready for him. Black Ivy says, if he's a problem, we'll just kill him. Elly doesn't know if she was kidding. She suspects not. Meanwhile, she has to get busy on the radio show. Ray wants her to be the producer. She's got to learn how. She's also wondering how many days they'll be in a Metric Week.

GLANCING GLASSES AND BODY MODIFICATIONS

BOG'S BEEN GIVING EVERYONE DIRTY LOOKS, but didn't know it. Like most of them, his eyes are getting worse and, although he's had reading glasses for a while, he finally had to breakdown and get his first pair of bifocals. They're completely round with a heavy black frame so that he looks like a cross between Buddy Holly and Mr. Peepers. He had a lot of trouble getting used to them, especially when trying to read something at eye level, like a computer monitor or a bulletin board notice. The trouble comes when trying to tip your head back far enough to get the reading lens at the right angle. He tried different solutions, like using a removable spacer under the nose bridge to elevate the lenses when needed. Then he came up with his lens rotation solution.

Because the lenses are perfectly round, he was able to loosen and unglue the frames and turn each lens ninety degrees clockwise (from his side) so that he could read at eye level by just turning his head to the right and looking out the left side, then reversing the routine for regular long distance vision. It took a little getting use to but he was starting to get along pretty well until he aggravated one of Ruby's guests. The source of the trouble comes when Bog looks at you through the right side of the lenses with his head cocked the other way, it looks like he's giving you a suspicious, sidelong glare. Bog thought he was politely listening to this couple at the Inn talk about their family but they didn't see it that way. They were offended by his apparent skeptical attitude and were so angry that they swore at him and checked out.

Meanwhile, things are moving ahead on Ray's radio setup. The rest of the equipment arrived a while ago and the boys have it hooked together and powered up. They're busy doing reception checks by continuously broadcasting a test signal and riding around the area to see how far the it goes. They should be on the air any day now. Black Ivy and Elly have been busy building up the music library and having fun shopping for CDs. At the same time, Monday Night Church is continuing and settling down to a predictable routine. They're filling up the place and usually have a few standing in the back. Ray's taking written questions now. They give everyone an index card as they come in and Louie collects them during the first song. Ray reviews them and picks the ones he wants to answer. The odd couple (the woman with horns and her ornamented friend) are still coming. They seem pleasant but Ray and Elly have been shaking hands with everyone at the door as they leave and thanking them for coming. When shaking hands with the tattooed boy, Elly noticed that he had about a two inch ring under the skin of his forearm. You could clearly see the outline of it. Elly's heard of these imbedded body ornaments before but she didn't think anyone around there would be doing it. Bog later says this is just the beginning, and pretty soon kids will be customizing their bodies like they customized their cars back in the fifties and sixties with scoops, fins, and fender skirts. Then he says, other people will start customizing their body for practical reasons, like forming a bracket on your upper arm to attach your cell phone or a hook on your waist to hold your key chain. Elly thought she could use a pair of Hershey Kiss sized points on the top of each shoulder to keep her straps up, although she might draw a few sidelong glances of her own.

ACTIVE RECEPTION

GOOD NEWS. Boolie's gone and the police are after him. After he healed up, he returned to the Cheshire Rake and Hoe office, still demanding his overtime pay, and quickly got into a hot argument with the Accounting manager's administrative assistant. He gave her a few bruises and busted up the office. The police came and hauled him off. He was supposed to appear in court the following week, but he didn't show up and now they can't find him. Meanwhile, they put Elly on "leave of absence," so she's still an employee and they said she can come back whenever she's ready. Orchard says they might be worried that she'd sue them. Elly doesn't think so. Nevertheless, she's not ready to return.

She's more interested in Ray, the Church and the radio program. The show's coming together fairly well. They've been broadcasting for almost a week and she's been having a thrill playing all the songs she likes. She finds the sense of power and control intoxicating. She keeps trying to imagine who's listening; of course, they don't know if anybody is. Too bad there's no device to determine how many radios are receiving your signal she thought. She'd think someone could come up with such a device. Ruby says the marketing people would really like it. Bog says the government probably already has some sort of reception detection equipment. He says they also probably have it tied in with their GPS system so they can tell where the signals are being received. He's probably right. She thinks she better make sure she doesn't get caught listening to Howard Stern.

Ray, however, doesn't seem to care how many people are tuned in. Each night he talks to the microphone as though there's only one person listening. You'd think he was sitting at a bar having a beer and a chat with someone. To support that notion, Elly's building up a tape of barroom background noises: people talking, laughing, glasses clinking, pool balls clicking, and so on, as well as music from a juke box. Then she'll play it throughout the whole broadcast. Ray's all for it, as long as she gets the levels right; it's got to be loud enough for the proper effect without interfering with his presentation. They're also equipped to take callers, but Ralph advised Ray to avoid it. He says that a lot of shows use callers to substitute for content; which can work, but it's hard to control. Kind of like Ray's question and answer session at church Elly supposed.

Monday Night services are still going okay but they're wondering how the radio show will affect the turn out. Ruby thinks it will drop attendance, since people can just stay home and listen to Ray, while Black Ivy thinks it will attract some younger people who'll want to see a live show.

Meanwhile, Bog has readjusted his bifocals to the normal position and is learning to deal with them; everyone feels better. Cheshire Rake and Hoe may also have to learn to deal with him. He drove Elly to the office a couple of days ago so she could pick up her check and a few personal things, (which is where she got all the information about Boolie). While waiting for her, Bog filled out a job application for a Quality Assurance Technician and even got an initial interview with the Human Resources lady. Elly supposed he could do the job but they have no idea what they'd be getting into. She doesn't know what she'll do if he lists her as a reference.

BOG'S JOBS

BOG GOT HIRED at Cheshire Rake and Hoe. They called him back for more interviews and hired him on as a second shift quality technician. He'll being working on the equipment that the inspectors use to test the products. They must have liked him, either that, or no one else applied. Also, knowing her might have helped. As Elly feared, they called her for a reference. She was as honest and as vague as possible. About the only specific thing she said was that he was perceptive and somewhat innovative. He starts next week (assuming the standard background check goes okay). Up until now, Bog's usually worked at home. He's got a small shop attached to the back of their house where he makes odds and ends and sells them at craft shows and fairs (he makes these silly little things out of wood with plastic tubes that toot; he calls them "Lumpy Monkey Whistles" and sells them for $5.00 each. Kids buy them). He says he'll continue to keep his home business active at some level, but he's more concerned about giving up his afternoon visits with Ruby.

Elly didn't think he'd care about someone keeping her company but he's worried enough about it that he asked Ray and her to fill in for him from time to time. Of course Elly's there already and Ray's over fairly often, but Bog says he feels that she needs someone to sit and listen to her for an hour or so each day. He says he's been doing it since Uncle Ollie died and that Ollie was a good listener and even told Bog how to do it. He says it's not as easy as it seems because you have to learn to resist the urge to offer advice, solve a problem, or debate. Mostly, he says, people just want your attention.

They agreed, but listening to Ruby is a little tricky. She often starts speaking in pronouns, as though she's begun the conversation earlier and you've come in late. It takes a while to figure out who or what she's complaining about, and asking her is apt to make her think you hadn't been paying attention. Elly had already gotten used to it and it didn't occur to her that anyone else was aware of it, but Bog was very aware of the problem and warned Ray. He says he deals with it by filling in the blanks to himself with his own nouns. He says it makes the whole story more interesting. Like the last time he was over, she started off saying "..if *he* thinks I'm going along with *that*, *he* can go to hell!"

"So," says Bog, "I imagined that the 'he' in the story was a chubby Persian with puffy purple pants swinging a pair of matching silver sabers in the backyard, and the 'that' he wants her to 'go along with' is a plan to trim the rhododendron bushes into the shape of giant weasels. Then, he says she continues: '...and there's no way I'm paying more than $4.00 a gallon for *it*!' So I shift gears and imagine this liquid is a load of ginger ale that the Persian is trying to sell to Ruby from a long tanker truck for a special Polish wedding reception she has to arrange. I just have to be careful that I don't slip up and let her know my version of her story," he says.

Now Elly finds herself being careful when talking to Bog. It makes her worry as to how *she's* being interpreted.

AIR TEXT

RAY'S BEEN HIRED AS A PERSONAL MINISTER. Since Bog started work, Ray, at Bog's request, has been spending a little time with Ruby nearly every afternoon before the radio show. Like Bog said, she seems to enjoy the attention. She also told one of her friends, a former dentist's wife, about Ray and had her come to Monday Night Church. Afterwards, the woman asked Ray if he'd make *house calls*. Ray took her seriously and without hesitating said "Sure," and made an appointment for the next day. He showed up and stayed for an hour; she paid him $20 and scheduled another appointment for next week. Ray said he answered a few of her questions, but, mostly, he just listened to her talk about her problems and concerns. He says he feels guilty about charging her for just listening, but she was happy to pay and even offered him more than he asked for. Orchard said he should charge at least $40 an hour. Bog says Ray should emulate *Brer Rabbit*'s scarecrow job and charge "a dollar a minute." Ruby says they should be charging Bog a dollar a minute for listening to his nonsense. She says she doesn't know how Black Ivy tolerates him. She's more patient than she seems but she's also happy about his job; says she'll be glad to get him out from under foot. She also says she'll continue with the banner towing business and she's even working on a scheme to expand the operation.

Bog had been nagging her to try *sky writing*. She says she didn't think her penmanship would be good enough and it would be hard on the plane. However, Louie came up with an alternate plan. Instead of one streaming vapor jet, he's working out an arrangement using seven jets and pulsing them. If he can pulse them fast enough, and if she can fly slow enough, he says she can write her messages like an old dot matrix printer, using a five by seven character pattern. She would simply fly along and puff out an array of smoke dots that would print out the message as though it were coming off a ticker tape machine. Louie has one jet attached under the center of the plane and three on each wing, spaced about four feet apart from each other. Black Ivy had made a few practice runs, leaving a random array of smoke dots in the sky. She says flying slow is very tricky because it's close to the *stall* speed, which is the point where the plane loses lift and falls out of the sky and, because she's not that high, there wouldn't be much time to get the plane under control. Things seem backwards with flying; Elly thought it would be better to go slow and close to the ground, but it turns out to be safer to go fast and fly high.

Meanwhile, the radio show's taking off pretty well. Elly has a fairly believable barroom din soundtrack that she plays in the background while Ray talks, then, when he's ready for a break, he acts like there's a live performance starting up; and then she plays two or three songs by the same artist (to give the illusion that they're actually right there on a small stage). After each song, she plays an applause sound track and it sounds like everyone's having a great time. It's hard to tell if it's affecting Monday Night Church; some of the familiar faces have gone but new people are showing up, including some college kids. Elly hopes Ray doesn't get talked into any "house calls" there.

AIR BORNE GRAFFITI AND AUDIENCE EVALUATION

THERE'S AN ARRAY OF WHITE DOTS IN THE SKY. Little round clouds forming a string of backward printed letters that seem to say: "GNITSET 321 GNITSET." Black Ivy's making the dots with her airplane. Louie has put together an electronic box he calls a "shift register" that they use to program pulses to the seven smoke jets for the vertical part of the five by seven dot matrix letters. They can key in up to 256 pulses which, allowing for spaces between the letters, lets them print out a thirty six character message. The characters were stretched out (sideways) quite a bit at first, but Louie repositioned the smoke jets as far apart as he could (on her 30 foot wing span) to increase the letter's height, and he sped up the pulse rate (as much as the jets would allow) to decrease the letters' width. Now the characters are still slightly stretched, but quite legible. Bog wanted Louie to add an eighth jet so that they could underline certain words, but they've run out of wing.

Black Ivy's looking for an easier way to code the messages because it's a lot of work. She has to lay it out on graph paper to be sure to get the dot sequence right, and to make it worse, it turns out that she'll have to key in the message backwards to keep it from coming out backwards. Like a car, she flies the plane from the left seat, and because she wants to keep the viewing target in sight on her left side as she's flying, she has to print the message from right to left so you see the ending before the beginning.

Monday Night Church is beginning to get a little more crowded. There are always several people standing in the back and a lot of people are coming early to get a seat. Ruby's begun to sing with Elly on some of the numbers, like they did when Ollie was running the show. She's actually pretty good; their version of *Once Upon a Time* by Rochelle and the Candles made a big hit. Elly even got Ray to join in and sing back-up base. Black Ivy thinks they ought to cut an album and call themselves *Ray and the Relics*. Ruby says she's been hanging around with Bog too long. Elly thought she'd be nervous with so many people watching them but, instead, she found herself watching *them*.

There's one fidgety middle aged guy with a wide white belt and brown plaid pants who always looks like he's about to explode into a passionate dialog about the virtues of vinyl siding. Bog thinks he's a pesticide salesman. The college kids are still coming; Elly catches them taking notes, which makes her think the church is being evaluated as part of some term paper. One of them always buys a DVD of the previous week's session from Orchard, even though he was there and saw the live show.

There're two well dressed men in their thirties or early forties who sit together. Elly's almost sure that, for a moment, she saw them holding hands. She tries to be open minded, but she still finds it very unsettling. There's also a stark looking older woman with a pale thin face, deeply set eyes separated by a sharp hooked nose. She doesn't talk and doesn't smile. She makes Ruby nervous. Orchard says she looks *hollow*. Black Ivy doesn't like her and says she looks like she's holding back dreadful secrets, as though she was the exwife of the grim reaper. Then again, Black Ivy takes a grim view of a lot of people.

MARITAL REVOLUTION

Elly THINKS THEY'LL NEED INSURANCE. After last Monday night's services, those gay men (the ones she saw holding hands) asked Ray to marry them. Ray politely declined and referred them to a place down in Massachusetts that's been doing it. Orchard says they'll probably be seeing more of this. Ruby agrees but says it'll be worse than it looks. She says that there's too much attention on the gay side of this. She says the real problem is *same sex* marriage, or more generally, the idea that anyone will be able to marry anyone they want. She says that after the gays blaze the trail and people get over the stigma of it, regular folks that don't want to have a family will be getting married just for the tax breaks. It'll start out with friends getting married but, eventually, there'll be agencies set up to arrange marriages over the internet and people won't even need to know the people they're marrying. Before you know it, Fox or someone will make a game show out of it. If that happens, Orchard says, there'll be a big distinction between civil ceremonies and church weddings, in that mothers will insist that their daughters have legitimate church weddings to separate them from the same sex sinners.

Since Bog and Black Ivy aren't married, Elly thought he'd lay low and keep quiet on this, but no, he jumps right in. He says Ruby's right about this just being the beginning but he thinks it will evolve differently. He says once the gay weddings become commonplace, the bisexual folks will say "what about us? We want to marry *both* of our partners!" Then, some well meaning State government like Vermont will give in and pass a law saying you can marry one of each sex. Actually, they'll repeal the polygamy law to allow dual sex bigamy. So the bisexuals will be allowed to go ahead and marry one of each. But soon the courts will say you can't specify sex in the law because it violates the new same-sex marriage laws. It won't take long for some guys to notice that it's legal to have two wives. After a few men get away with this, the women will realize that it applies to them too and they can have two husbands. This will lead to marriage "strings," where a woman will be married to two men, who, in turn, are also married to other women who are also married to other men, and so on. These strings would easily become a dozen or more people long, and in some cases, the two ends of the string will marry, creating a marriage "ring." They'll have big reunions and be eligible for group insurance benefits. Of course, someone will have to be the leader of the string or ring, so they'll have elections which will lead to the usual political problems and, ultimately, opposing sides. But, later, it'll all get complicated when someone eventually says, "If I can have two spouses, why not three?" There'll be a lot of debates and arguments but the politicians will finally compromise and set the limit at four. Four spouses, any gender (leading to quintessential weddings). But then, the marriage strings or rings will become interconnected and multi-dimensional such that nearly everyone would be linked one way or another by marriage. Ray didn't have much to say, but he agreed with Orchard's prediction that church marriages will become more important while civil marriages will degenerate to just a legal formality, no more important than a fishing license. Ruby says the divorce lawyers will make a fortune.

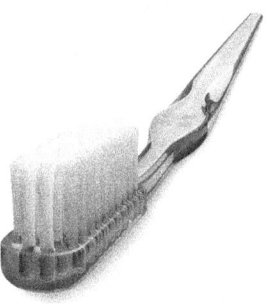

PERSONAL PROPERTY AND SPIRITUAL INCOME

SOMEONE MOVED ELLY'S TOOTHBRUSH. She doesn't know why anyone would need to move it and she can't help but wonder if it was used for anything in the process. She bought another.

Nevertheless, it reminds her that she should be getting her own place. She knows Ruby would let her stay there indefinitely, but she's still a house guest and she knows can only take that so far. On the other hand, she doesn't want to be alone; she's hoping Ray will decide to give up his illegal motor home and they could get a little place together.

Monday Night Church is starting to get even more crowded and they're having to turn people away. They're thinking of doing two shows; one at 7:00 and a second at 9:00. Orchard's DVD sales are also picking up quite a bit (Elly thinks it's because of the music). Further, he's been recording the radio show and getting set up to sell CDs. He gives her and Ray half of what he takes in; the rest goes into the church fund; actually, it all goes to the church then they get paid from that account.

At the same time, Ray's house call ministry (or home listening) business is picking up. He sees the dentist's wife once a week and a few other women have heard about the deal and hired him on for at least one visit. At Orchard's suggestion, Ray set his rate higher for new clients. As before, Ray answers a few of their questions but mostly just listens to them talk about whatever's bothering them, with one exception.

The hollow woman (with the hooked nose) also hired Ray. Actually her niece set up the appointment. But, like at church, the woman doesn't talk. Ray goes there; she motions for him to sit at the kitchen table and brings him coffee and a biscuit but doesn't sit with him. She continues to work in the kitchen while he sits there. To break the silence, he talks a little bit and she occasionally nods or lightly shakes her head; enough that Ray's pretty sure she's not deaf. After an hour, she got her purse, paid him and walked him to the door. On the way, she stopped at a calendar in the foyer and pointed to a Friday on the following month. Ray said: "Okay, I'll be here at ten?" The woman nodded. He said goodbye, she nodded again and closed the door.

Ruby does more than nod her head. Ray's still been coming over almost daily and listens to her. She's had a lot to complain about (Bog's puffy Persian turned out to be the heating oil man who's been raising his prices each time he comes). But, she's slowing down a bit; almost as though she's getting near the bottom of her sixty year long list of residual infractions. At least she seems more relaxed than Elly's ever seen her; she's almost happy.

Black Ivy's also happy. Her sky printing set up is working and she's already got some paying customers. Louie's working on the electronics so that they'll be able to key in the messages from a computer (instead of by hand) and he's increasing the memory so that they can handle longer and multiple messages. Bog says she'll be able to print out whole paragraphs. Black Ivy says he's probably right, as long as there's not much wind. She thinks she could do as many as four lines (there's not as much room to work with as you'd think; because the letters are small, she flies at a much lower altitude than conventional sky writers. Elly thinks she should have her spell out:

"WHO MOVED MY TOOTH BRUSH!".

HANDICAP HEAT

BOG'S ON CRUTCHES and Ruby's paying for it. At work, they have a lock on the employee entrance that uses a *proximity* switch. You just have to wave your badge within a few inches of the card reader, and the door unlocks. The card reader is a small box mounted on the outside wall, near the door; some people have their badges attached to their belt with these retractable key chains so they don't have to unclip it, taller people with belts just nudge up to the reader to get in, which is convenient when you're hands are full. Bog's hands are often full but he's not that tall, so when he has to carry something into work, he puts the badge in the cuff of his sock (until he gets to his desk). To unlock the door, he swings his foot high in the air, near the reader and "click," he's in. Well, anyone could see this coming; last week, in mid kick with his hands full of folders, his other foot slips and down he goes with an ugly twist. His ankle's not broken but he has to stay off it for a week.

For the first few days, Black Ivy rented a wheel chair and either she or Louie would wheel him around while he would hold the ramp boards. These boards are for the step or two at their house, the church and the Inn. Bog would carry them in his lap; when they came to a step, they'd lay them down to make a ramp over the steps, push him up, (which wasn't as easy as it sounds) then hand the boards back to him. By the third day, he was out of the chair and hobbling around on crutches well enough on his own, so they returned the chair. Trouble is, some concerned citizen must have seen the portable ramp arrangement during the first two days and complained to the State authorities.

A few days later, two women from the Disability Access Department showed up with a camera and a tape measure and gave Ruby a citation for not having a ramp for handicap access to the Inn. She's ripping mad. Orchard says she could fight it and probably get an exemption. But she'd rather fight with Bog; she's making *him* build the ramp. Louie's helping. They're making it out of pressure treated wood.

Having a ramp is probably not a bad idea anyway. The inn's been getting a little busier; it seems that the show at church is attracting a few people, or, at least, bringing some attention to the Inn.
They're going ahead with the dual Monday Night sessions. Black Ivy offered to advertise the new schedule with her sky printing setup, but Ruby's afraid it will attract more people and she says they're having enough trouble manage those they've already got.

Ray's managing his listening business reasonably well, with repeat customers lining up. One of the women (they're all women) is a fast talker, once Ray gets seated, she breaks into a rapid fire stream of complaints and gossip. It's as though she's trying to get the most spoken she can for the money. Ray says it wears him out and he's looking for ways to avoid her.

This reminded Black Ivy that Carla's become a bit of a big talker. She's at the age where she's learning a lot and needs to let you know it. Black Ivy asked Bog to come up with a way to slow her down a bit. It's a risky request but she's used to taking chances.

SIGNS OF SPEECH

THE HOLLOW WOMAN *SPOKE* TO CARLA. Carla, unlike the hollow woman, has been talking a lot and Bog (at Black Ivy's request) came up with a scheme to slow her down. It's a "Word Budget" arrangement.

While she's home from school, he allows her sixty words an hour, or one word a minute. She can borrow up to one hour's worth of words, but no more and she has to be paid up by bedtime. She keeps a word list, or daily transcript that Bog reviews each night. Elly's surprised that Carla's going along with it. The scheme has had an immediate effect and is almost working *too* well; she chooses her few words very carefully and has learned to get along without adverbs, adjectives and articles. She's also resorted to conventional body language where possible (like shaking her head or waving her arms). But, she couldn't come up with gestures for simple things like "I'm sorry," "Excuse me" or "Can I go to Stanley's house?" So she got on the Web and dug up a bunch of information on *sign language*. She's learned a few gestures, but nobody else knows what she's saying, *almost* nobody.

At the close of Monday Night Church, while waiting for Bog and her mother, she was practicing her "How are You?" gesture as people were coming out, and the hollow woman *answered*: "I'm fine," in sign language. It happened to be one of the few gestures that Carla recognized because it's a funny little finger wiggling motion. The woman made a few other gestures but Carla could only respond by shrugging her shoulders. Then, with a worried face, the woman asked her outright: "Can you hear?" Carla used one of her sixty words and said "Yes." The woman smiled, said "Good for you," patted her on the head and left. Elly can't wait to see how Ray's next visit with her goes.

At the other extreme, Ray's been successfully avoiding the fast talking woman by getting new customers scheduled ahead of her; more than he knows what to do with. He has an appointment book, just like a dentist uses, and has sessions scheduled as far as two months ahead. Except for the first four women, he's charging $40 an hour. Orchard says this could be a whole new industry if you could get doctors to prescribe *listening* and insurance companies to pay for it.

Elly wishes they could get paid for the radio show. She's increased the music inventory such that they've added two hours to the front end of the broadcast. They don't have the phone number listed and they've explicitly said "no requests" but people keep mailing them in anyway. So, instead, they're accepting *negative* requests. That is, if Elly plays a song that the listener just can't stand (forcing them to change the channel) they can send in a request to have her stop playing it; and if they get enough negative requests for a song, Elly ceremoniously burys it. She's had to kill one so far (*Blue Monday* by the Fats Domino). It was one Elly liked, so she's not happy about dropping it. Music is a tricky business. Nobody likes all the same songs that you like, but most everyone wants you to like all the dreadful songs that they like. Elly remembered that it used to always be a source of conflict on the production floor at work. People would really start to hate other workers, because of the music they played. She hopes this I-Pod craze will help people keep their awful music to themselves.

BUS BOYS AND RADIO RELICS

BOG BOUGHT A BUS. A big yellow school bus. It's a twelve year old Thomas on a Ford chassis with a diesel engine in the back. He paid cash so Elly doesn't think it cost too much. They don't know what he's up to but Louie seems to be in on it. They have it parked behind Louie's garage where they've been busy taking the seats out and they're also getting it ready for a paint job. It looks like trouble to her. Ruby's all tensed up about it and constantly keeping an eye on them but doesn't say anything. Before bringing in the bus, Bog and Louie finished the Inn's handicap ramp and did a pretty good job, so Elly thinks Ruby feels conflicted and doesn't want to confront him about anything just yet.

Bog's *Word Budget* scheme for Carla is also finished and she's talking again. It turned out that she handled the project very well and even over did it to the point where the silence drove Black Ivy crazy. She had to make Carla stop (or start talking again) by saying she "Won the Prize." And brought her to up to the Concord Mall to get it: a bright red Bolivian shepherd's hat (at least that's what Black Ivy called it) with a wide brim and yellow fringe around the edge; it's been three days and Carla hasn't stopped wearing it. Ruby told her that she looks like a *Spanish Princess*. Bog, on the other hand, calls her a *Cuban Cowgirl*. But, she's still a fairly quiet cowgirl so they guess the exercise was somewhat successful.

Elly's been playing cuts from the Monday Night Church recordings on the radio and the manager of a Blues club in Keene heard it and called around and eventually found her at the Inn. She asked who the performers were. Elly didn't want to give her their names, so she blurted out the first thing that popped into her head: "Ray and the Relics" (Black Ivy's nick name for them). The woman took her seriously and asked a lot of questions about the group. If Elly can talk Ray and the other Relic into it, they have a booking for a two hour show a week from Wednesday.

Meanwhile, they're doing the double Monday night shows at Church. The first session fills up as usual and a few people are still standing in the back but not as many as before. Instead, they wait for the second show where they get about half as big a crowd which includes a few people form the first show that stay to hear it twice. Ray's uneasy about just repeating the same sermon so he mixes it up a bit. Also, no one with kids is hanging around for the second session so he has to skip the usual kid story and fills in with more local or national news analysis.

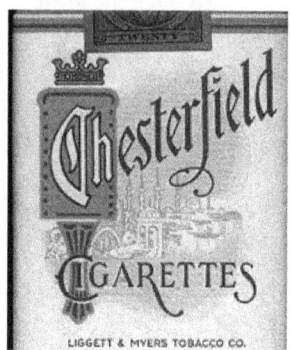

During the second sermon, Elly was busy watching the ornamented couple who brought an ornamented friend; a tattooed girl with nearly normal hair but some kind of cheek ring. It looked like a miniature thimble right on the side of her face with the open end sticking outward.

It turned out to be a cigarette holder with a thin tube going through her cheek into her mouth. After the show, on her way out the door, she stuck in a Chesterfield, lit up and left in a cloud of smoke. Lips and hands free.

Elly thinks they could sell tours to this place. Perhaps that's what Bog's yellow bus is for.

SINGING THE BLUES

E LLY'S PISSED. Both Ray and Ruby rejected the idea of singing at the Blues club. Neither of them even thought it over. She asked them separately but they both just quickly said no. She was all excited about it but now she's disappointed and mad. She expected trouble from Ruby but Ray's rejection was a surprise, he's usually pretty agreeable but, this time, he wasn't even sympathetic. He said wanting things too much causes trouble; a week ago she was happy he says, but now, she's made herself miserable only because she wanted something; something she didn't know she wanted the week before. She hopes he doesn't think that's suppose to make her feel better, and how does he know what *she* doesn't want. She's added the Rolling Stones' *You Can't Always Get*

What You Want to her play list; it helps her sulk.

Ruby's not sulking but she's pretty wound up. At the moment, all she wants is to keep an eye on Bog and his bus. He and Louie finished taking all of the seats out and they're busy putting in thin plywood for a sub flooring. He's also got several boxes of those adhesive backed linoleum floor tiles ready to go. At the same time, Louie has started painting the outside. He's got a gas-powered air compressor that he's using to spray on a high gloss, robin's egg blue lacquer for a base coat with wispy looking cirrus like clouds scattered down the sides. No one still has any idea of what they're up to, except that there's a movie screen and what looks like a podium involved.

When Louie's not working on the bus, he's been hanging around at the station with Elly late in the afternoon while she plays music before Ray goes on the air. He's very interested in the audio editing equipment she uses to put soundtracks together (like the ambient barroom effect and others). It's just a computer program on a PC (they're using an old IBM that Orchard had left over after upgrading to his new DVD burning Dell). She showed Louie how she can clip, copy, modify, and repeat the smallest segments (from any source that she can find) to a WAV file. She can change voice recordings too; she has one of Ray where she raises the pitch (without increasing the speed) such that he ended up sounding like a thin old lady. They're thinking of putting together mock interviews with themselves. Between the two of them, she can come up with at least six separate voices.

Louie says this sounds similar to the computer graphics technology. He thinks that, since computer generated graphics made movies such as *Jurassic Park* and *Lord of the Rings* possible, the same approach could be applied to make computer generated music. He saw in a documentary of how they created an army of Orcs by copying, pasting, and replicating the images of just a few actors. He thinks they could take a few odds and ends from her music library then modify and replicate them and piece together enough material to make a complete song. He's already started, using segments from Little Richard songs. But, instead of using the drums for a beat, he's using trumpets. Keep in mind that they can repeat whatever they want so any sharp sound does it. And he's also putting together snips of Freddy Mercury vocals along with various Patsy Cline cuts. Elly wonders if he could piece together a couple of singers that she could take to the Blues club.

MOBIL MEETINGS AND AIRBORNE MESSAGES

R UBY SAID THIS WOULD HAPPEN. Someone copied Ivy's sky printing method and they're doing it better. They've got a twin engine Beechcraft with a vertical boom off the tail holding the seven vapor jets one above the other which are also angled to fan out the dots, producing a much larger character than Black Ivy can. Also, being vertical, the characters are much more legible than her flat pattern.

Nevertheless, Louie has improved Black Ivy's message entry setup significantly. Not only can they code in the messages from the computer, they can program up to eight messages in the shift register at the house, then just bring it to the plane and plug it in. Also, Louie's looking for a used laptop so that she can take the whole setup and program real time messages while she's flying. It would be too dangerous for Black Ivy to try to do the typing so the plan is to get a second pair of headsets and bring Carla with her. Louie would relay from the ground, over the plane's radio frequency while Carla listens, then she would type the message (she can already type with all ten fingers) and Black Ivy would send it to the vapor jets. They're wondering what the Beechcraft will do to counteract the coding scheme. Nevertheless, Black Ivy says she'll keep at it and see how the competition evolves.

Meanwhile, Bog's bus has evolved and there's printing on the sides; big blue slanted letters that say: "Cloud Nine Conference Haul." It turns out that they've been building a "mobile meeting room" where the inside is one big open space. The plan is to advertise to local outfits and offer a conference room for companies or organizations that don't have an available location to hold a meeting or host a small function when they need one, especially on short notice. Bog and Louie had an open house (or open bus) for everyone last weekend. They were dressed in coats and ties and both of Louie's Ukrainian girlfriends, with their high heels and sharp accents, were the hostesses.

The tile floor looked good. The side windows are painted on the outside with a black undercoat so that they're like mirrors on the inside. They've got DC powered florescent lighting and a DC to AC inverter to operate an overhead projector and other small appliances. They've still got some work to do, like installing a roof air conditioning unit and a propane powered refrigerator. For furniture, they got a collection of chairs and eight five-foot folding tables, from a used office supply place in Brattleboro, which they can put together to make one big conference table, or line them up in rows, like a classroom. At first, Elly thought he was planning on "rolling meetings" where they would ride around someplace as people were having a conference inside, but, instead, they'll drive to the customer's location and park the bus right in their lot for the meeting. For now, Louie's the driver since he's the only one with a license to run it. But Bog's studying up for *his* CDL test at the Motor Vehicles Department.

Carla said they wouldn't need schools anymore, just a lot of classroom busses and a parking lot. Ray's first thought was using it for a mobile church. He could drive it to Hampton and have seaside services for the people who'd want to go to the beach and church at the same time. Ruby says they could use it for the waiting room for the second session of Monday Night Church. Elly wonders If anyone will copy this.

THE DEFENSE REALLY RESTS

ORCHARD'S DEAD. He was almost eighty. Ruby, Ray and Elly were sitting with him on the front porch of the Inn having their Sunday smoke. Orchard had been quiet and seemed uncomfortable. Ray and Ruby began talking about Church business; Elly was expecting Orchard to comment, but, instead, she heard his pipe hit the floor. She thought he just dropped it. His eyes were open, but he didn't move. Ruby checked him and Ray quickly called someone. Elly was stunned and frozen in her chair. Ruby closed his eyes then went in and got a sheet and covered him up, still sitting.

The ambulance came and packed him up and left with their sirens quiet. Ruby notified his two sons in Connecticut. They've made their way to the house in a day and have been making the arrangements. Orchard'll be buried in the Church's graveyard, next to his wife, Flo, who died about twelve years ago. Everyone's pretty depressed; except

Ruby. Although she loved Orchard, she seems to accept his passing with her usual resolve, like any other milestone or event that has to be dealt with.

Elly felt like it was a big event; not only did she feel bad about losing him, it was also a grim reminder of how temporary all this is. Here she was, in the last half, well, the last third of her life, but where was she? Who'll remember that she was here? She thought Orchard could have said the world was a little better off because he was here, but Elly didn't think she could say the same. She can't think of more than a few who'd miss her, and she kept thinking of the theme from one of Ray's roadside sermons where he asked: *Who'll be Happy When You're Gone?* Orchard's two sons won't be happy when they learn that he turned over his property to the Church's trust.

Ruby also notified Orchard's lawyer, which seemed odd to Elly that *he'd* have an attorney, but the attorney's also the executor of the estate. They know Orchard updated his will when he set up the Church trust but they don't know if he did anything about naming who'd run it in his place. Elly assumed Ray would be in charge, but Ray doesn't think so. He said they hadn't talked about it but he's sure Orchard would have planned on something. It's a legal entity, so they're all pretty sure that the operation has to survive.

The general thought is that they'll expand the Bed and Breakfast business to include Orchard's house. There's four bedrooms upstairs and a big downstairs, with a full parlor, as well as large living and dining rooms. Ruby says they might even build an enclosed walkway between the two buildings. Everyone seems to be looking ahead, but Elly can't think about it. She must have been moping around enough for Ray to notice. He spent some time with her to talk it over. He says it's hard for us to deal with death; not just because we've lost a loved one, but the whole concept of death is hard to accept. He says that we owe our existence to a genetically intense *will to live,* but this *will* also forces us to deny the inevitability of our own death. This creates a conflict and leads to dreams of heaven and a vast array of religious revelations, but, once you discover the source of the conflict, you can find peace and the anxiety subsides. Elly doesn't feel that she's anxious about anything, She's just depressed and he's not helping.

TAKE ME OUT OF THE BALL GAME

ELLY SWALLOWED A BUG. She was visiting Black Ivy last Sunday and they were outside pulling weeds out of her flower bed. There she was, with her mouth wide open, laughing about something Bog did, when in it went. A small fly or gnat she thinks. They went inside and washed it down with some Cabernet Sauvignon.

Bog and Carla were there, watching a baseball game. Black Ivy was surprised. Like her mother, Carla's a big baseball fan but she says Bog wasn't interested and never watched. The session went something like this:

    Shot of the batter.

    Bog: "He spit!"

    Carla: "It's okay, pay attention."

    Bog: "Basketball players don't spit."

A couple of more pitches and he lines out hard to the short stop.

Bog: "It's a *Hit to the Mitt*!"

Carla: "There's no such thing as a *Hit to the Mitt*, you're thinking of a *Tip to the Mitt*."

Bog: "That's a *tip*?"

Carla: "No! I'll show you when it happens."

The next batter eventually pops out to Second Base.

Bog: "Was that a *Tip to the Mitt*?"

Carla: "No, that was a *Pop-up*."

Later on, another batter grounds out to Third.

Bog: "That must have been a *Pop down*."

Carla: "No! That was a *Ground out*! Just listen to the announcer."

Another pop up.

Bog: "That should be an *Air out*."

After a few hits, they brought in a new Pitcher.

Bog: "A *Pinch Pitcher*!"

Carla: "He's a *Relief* Pitcher. You're thinking of a *Pinch Runner* or a *Pinch Hitter*."

Later, the batter was introduced as the *Designated Hitter*.

Bog: "Who's the *Designated Pitcher*."

Carla: No response.

Bog: "How about the Catcher; is there a *Designated Catcher*?"

Carla: "There's only *Designated Hitters*!" Carla explained the American League's batting rules. This led to a big argument about whether they should or shouldn't have Offensive and Defensive teams (nine hefty batters and a separate bunch of wiry strong armed men for the field).

Bog: "They ought to get Football managers to run these games."

The next batter is introduced as a *Switch Hitter*. The Catcher goes to the mound for a conference with the Pitcher.

Bog (seeming to catch on): "Do they have *Switch Pitchers* for the *Switch Hitters*."

Carla: "No! There's only *Switch Hitters*!"

The camera stays on the Pitcher as the Catcher returns to the plate.

Bog: "The Pitcher spit! Right on the mound!"

Carla: "Sometimes they spit."

Bog: "Hockey players don't spit."

The batter gets hit by the pitch in the leg and goes to First. Bog is surprised that he gets on base just for getting hit. Later, with a runner on Third and two outs, they intentionally walk the batter. Bog is again surprised. Carla explained the strategy.

Bog: "Why doesn't the Pitcher just *hit* him on purpose? He could just toss the ball lightly right at him; it'd be easier and quicker." Carla thinks about it but doesn't respond.

A shot of the stands as a *wave* passes through the crowd from the third base side. Bog is astonished: "What's that?!"

Carla explains the custom: "It happens all the time," she said.

After another batter grounds out, Bog wonders: "What if a wave starts at opposite sides at the same time? What happens when they meet in the middle?"

Carla remains quiet.

A shot of the dugout.

Bog: "He spit! The *manager* spit! Right on the floor!"

Carla: "There's no floor; it's dirt."

Bog: "The *manager* spit; he's setting a bad example."

Carla: "They *all* spit."

Bog: "No wonder."

The game was tied in the seventh inning. Carla said she had homework to do and went upstairs. Bog watched the batter get a single and knock in a run. Then he got up headed outside.

"Aren't you going to watch the rest of the game?" Elly asked.

"It's no fun by yourself," he said.

Elly and Black Ivy got the rest of the wine and watched the end of the game by themselves. Elly noticed that the players *do* spit a lot. Black Ivy says they're probably getting rid of bugs in their mouth.

BOG'S THE BOSS

RUBY PRAYS FOR BOG. Ray doesn't do any praying during Monday Night Church and Elly knows it bothers Ruby; enough that she comes in once in a while and does her own praying. Elly was cleaning up by the piano while Ruby was there and overheard her praying. She also prayed for Orchard.

His services went fairly well. The funeral home was very elegant and the director was exceptionally pleasant, but, outside in their driveway (next to the regular one they used for Orchard) they had a silver *stretch* hearse. Ray looked at it for a while and estimated that it was long enough to hold two caskets, end to end; either that, or there was extra seating in there (the windows were tinted). Whatever the purpose, they agreed that, it didn't seem right.

Ray spoke at the funeral and did all right; Elly thought he'd make them cry, but, actually, they left feeling pretty good. Unlike Orchard sons, who have also left, but unhappy and empty-handed. The lawyer is settling the estate, everything (furniture, equipment, cash and his truck) is going to the Ollie Khan Church Trust; his boys got nothing. They're especially upset that the house had been transferred to the Church because they already had a realtor lined up to sell it. After hearing the bad news, they implied that they'd fight it in court, but Ruby says not to worry and that it's a *done deal* because Orchard was very specific and careful to set up all the transfers correctly. He was also specific in naming *Bog* as the Church's Trustee. Elly thought sure it'd be Ray or Ruby, but Bog is Ollie's nephew so she guesses that must have been Orchard's reasoning. Thinking back at the funeral, she could almost imagine that he was laying there with a little grin under his mustache.

Bog's not making any arrangements for running the Church yet, other than getting Louie to agree to run the technical side of things (recording the services, producing the DVDs and so forth), which leaves Bog with the job of collecting the Question and Answer cards during the opening song.

Louie's already familiar with the equipment and knows what to do. He's also helping Elly get set up for live broadcasts of the service (just the second show). He's also glad to have something to do to get his mind off of the Ukrainian girlfriends.

He had to break up with them because they got into an argument (with each other) which forced Louie to cut them loose. He says each of them wanted to continue on their own, but, although he misses them, he says it's all or nothing. Elly thinks that one girlfriend would be better than none, but he insists on two (never three by the way). She asked Ray why he thought Louie was that way; after-all, Louie's not a ladies' man or anything like that. Ray says that, if he had to guess, Louie was probably afraid of women. Elly told him that didn't make sense; why would he want *any* girlfriends if he was afraid of them, let alone two. Ray says that any *one* woman can be dangerous, but two probably keep each other in check, minimizing the risk. Elly's not sure how she feels about that, but no body's keeping her in check, so she thinks Ray better be careful what he says. Perhaps Ruby should pray for both Louie and Ray while she's at it. Elly later told Bog that Ruby prays for him. He says he knows. Says he counts on it.

HIGHER AND HIRED

THE HOLLOW WOMAN'S AN ARTIST, and she's giving Ray lessons. Ray decided not to charge her for his visits (since he doesn't do much more than just sit with her for the hour) so, instead, she suggested (she actually spoke) that he accept some art instruction. He agreed and he's already learned the basic shading techniques. He had been busy drawing spheres and cylinders, but has moved on to faces. He's making progress but still has a long way to go.

The rest of his home preaching (or home listening) business is also progressing. With twelve regular clients, he stopped accepting new customers, but he has a waiting list of four additional women (including the fast talking woman). Again, it's only women, mostly older women but there's at least one in her thirties. Elly doesn't know how many of them are married but some of them must be. He expects some will start dropping off, then he'll fill in with the new women, but, none have stopped yet.

Monday Night Church is showing no signs of slowing down. Louie's running the recording equipment and they're also broadcasting the second show, which is now just a full as the first show. New people are showing up, including the manager of *Loamer's* (the blues club that had offered them the singing job last month). She called and said she saw the performance and offered Elly a solo gig at the club. So she's going over there Tuesday to check out their setup and equipment, including a high tech keyboard; if things look okay, she'll be on for two hours each Sunday afternoon. She'll also have to get her picture taken for the promotional material. Ruby's worried about drunken men and made her promise to be careful. She's also concerned about her using the family name, but Elly thinks she'll try a stage name and is thinking of using *Rachael Angle* (not *Angel*). She knows what people will think: "What's *that* suppose to mean?" Well, nothing, just something that's easy to say and sticks in your head. But, the idea of a new name is not far from a new identity; it gets you thinking. Ray likes the idea, he calls her "a *cute* angle," and says he'll come and watch. Louie also wanted to come and record a DVD of the show, but it's not allowed.

Meanwhile, he's been busy in the studio working on his computer generated music experiments. He's come up with some interesting segments, but nothing you could call a song yet. He's also been busy with Black Ivy and Carla and the sky printing business.

Carla's on the payroll too. It works like this: Carla rides with Black Ivy, Louie stays on the ground and mans the phone. A call comes in with a message request, Louie gets the credit card information and relays the message to Carla over the radio, Carla types it in on the laptop (on her lap), Black Ivy reads the screen and confirms the text with Louie,

Carla downloads the message to the shift register box, and Black Ivy sends it to the vapor jets at the right moment. Callers can have their message displayed in the air within a minute. So far, they've got a lot of "HAPPY BIRTHDAY ..." *so and so*, and "CONGRATULATIONS ..." *such and such a team* and things like that. They've also got a few requests for some profane and some somewhat questionable messages; so they have to be careful of what they accept. Black Ivy's still worried about the competition but says she'll keep at it, as long as it pays off. If not, she says she'll try something else.

SLIPPERY SLOPES

RUBY'S MADDER THAN A WET CAT. The State rejected the Inn's new handicap ramp. It's one degree too steep. Doesn't sound like much but it has to be completely rebuilt. Some of the lumber can be reused, but not all. Bog, Louie, and Ray are working on it now. While they're at it, they're going to build a covered walkway between Ruby's and Orchard's house.

As planned, they're adding Orchard's house to the Inn. They'll convert the downstairs half bath to a full bathroom and set up the parlor, living and dining rooms as bedroom suites. This will create a total of seven new rooms to rent out. They've been busy cleaning the place up for several days now. Ruby's mailing anything that appears personal to his sons. They've also uncovered a vast collection of *door knobs*, all kinds: glass, crystal, brass, iron, ceramic and porcelain, perhaps two hundred of them. Orchard never displayed them or showed them to anyone. Ruby thinks they might have been some form of payment from one of his poorer clients (it's anybody's guess). They were in wooden crates in his study which they've cleaned out for both Bog and Louie to use as an office to run the Trust and to produce the Church service DVDs. Elly tried to talk Ray into moving into one of the upstairs bedrooms, but he says he'll stay in the camper (she think he's an *incurable* hobo). Ruby's not feeling quite as charitable, she'd rather move him to the doghouse at the moment. She's mad about his recent wedding rejection.

A nice young smiling couple in their early twenties (a straight couple this time) waited outside until the end of services last Monday and asked Ray if he could marry them at the Church a month from now. He brought them back inside to talk it over and had Elly sit in on the meeting. It was like an interview. Their situation was fairly unremarkable. They were already living together, but wanted to make their relationship legitimate (mostly for their parents' peace of mind) and to, perhaps, have children. Ray listened and had a few questions and right at the point where Elly expected him to say: "Sure, we'd be glad to." He said he'd rather have them think it over for a while. He explained that there's too much pressure on young people to get married, and particularly too much pressure to have children. He says we're given the impression that it's our social, moral obligation, or duty to raise families but it's actually just nature's plot to perpetuate the species. He says we don't *have* to, and suggested that it's okay to resist these internal forces and that these forces are only providing motivation for the overall well being of the human race but they're not necessarily favorable for the individuals directly involved. So he asked them to examine other marriages (that they feel are successful) and to evaluate their own true goals in life, and he warned them not to let society *or* nature control of them. Then said he'd be glad to talk to them again, in perhaps, three months.

The boy seemed puzzled, the girl left crying. Elly thought it was rotten. Ruby agreed and told him so, but Black Ivy (who refused to marry Carla's father) wasn't so quick to condemn him. She said she'd need to think about it a little more. Ruby has no doubts and says young people should just do the right thing and that the State should forget about her handicap ramp and reject Ray's Minister's License instead.

DRAWN AND REFORMED

ELLY'S ALL SET to start singing at the Blues Club next Sunday. She'll need twelve to fourteen songs for the set. They have an electronic keyboard, so all she needs to bring is her harmonica and rack. Her name will be _Patty Angle_ (the manager thought "Rachael" was too folksy. She went over there a few days ago to work out the details and to the sign the contract (it's good for three months). They also took several promotional photographs of her for the poster and brochures and let her choose the one she liked best; but, in all of them, she thought she looked too old. So, instead, Ray took her to the hollow woman for a portrait. She drew a very simple pen and ink caricature of her face. Elly guessed it was okay. The hollow woman didn't sign it and didn't ask Elly if she liked it; she didn't talk to her at all. The session was kind of spooky; Elly's glad Ray was there. He says the drawing looks great, everybody else seems to like it all right. They took it to the club; the manager thought it was fine and said it would reproduce well. Black Ivy says it makes her look mysterious, Bog says she looks like someone famous.

But then, he's in a better than usual mood. He and Louie finished installing the propane air conditioner on the mobile function room bus (the *Cloud Nine Conference Haul*) and they're in business. They've already had their first customer: a small medical equipment manufacturer holding an employee outing up in the White Mountains. All the employees rode up in a separate bus and Louie met them there. The company held some sort of motivational meeting in the bus's room but, mostly, they just used it as a lounge for people who weren't out hiking or seeing the sights. The problem Louie hadn't planned on, was figuring out what to do with himself when they're using the bus. He had to make himself scarce, but there was no where to go. So he just walked around with nothing to do but read tourist pamphlets. Apart from that, it all went well and they paid on the spot.

Ray's finally picking up some business too. Some spin-off of the Presbyterians called the "North Calvinites" hired him for two Sundays up in Hanover. It's a small outfit with roughly 50 parishioners. Elly worries about these off-the-wall outfits, you never know what sort of bizarre beliefs they might have. She read about one group (not too far from there) who claim that the world is only 6,000 years old and they still insist that it's mostly flat (just curved a little, like a frisbee). They're also proponents of the old Julian calendar, believing that the Gregorian Calendar is a sinister Vatican scheme to bend time. Ray says he's fairly comfortable with people like that because you don't have to debate them about anything and they don't have any questions. He says, it seems, the wackier the religion, the more adamant and resolute the believers are; almost as though there's a formula at work. Nevertheless, she said he should avoid the wacky ones; he said he couldn't, says they're *all* wacky, to some degree. Anyway, she told him she was worried, but he says the Calvins are simple reformers (actually reformers of reformers) and reformers, although they can be a little touchy, are usually not too dangerous. Elly offered to come with him for musical support. He said she better not, he heard that they're skeptical of musicians, especially famous old folk singers.

STANLEY STINKER

ELLY HAS HER FAIR SHARE OF GRAY HAIR and was complaining about it while visiting Black Ivy. "Does that mean your dying?" asks an impertinent little boy from the corner of the kitchen. It was Carla's friend, Stan. Before Elly could protest, Black Ivy jumped in: "It means she's as fierce as a wolf and knows just what to do with little stinkers like you, now get out of here!" Carla grabbed his hand and dragged him out of Ivy's reach. On their way outside, Carla admonished him further: "You know better than to try that when my Mom's around, she said she'd fry you raw next time!"

Once they were out of ear shot, Black Ivy warned Elly that he was testing her and that she should be careful. She said he's the kind of boy who would tell an anorexic girl that she looks "chubby." His technique is to find your weaknesses, fears, or source of anxieties then exploit them just for the fun of tormenting you. Not long ago, he drove Louie near the edge of insanity with his Suduko scam.

Like many people, Louie is addicted to the puzzles and can't resist trying to solve them. Stan picked up on this and began, once a week, leaving copies of difficult ones that he found on the web where Louie would find them. Louie would eventually solved them, but then, Stan began alternately leaving doctored versions imbedded with an error such that the puzzle couldn't be solved. Louie was pulling his hair out. No one would have known what was going on if Carla hadn't spilled the beans. Elly asked Black Ivy if she had been a victim, Black Ivy said 'no,' says she never lets anyone know what she's afraid of or cares about, instead, she has Stan a little worried and convinced that she knows a few Cuban Voodoo tricks and gives the impression she wouldn't hesitate to turn him into a stuttering zombie while he's sleeping.

Nevertheless, she said it's critical for Elly that Stan knows nothing about Boolie, there's no telling how he'd exploit a fear like that.

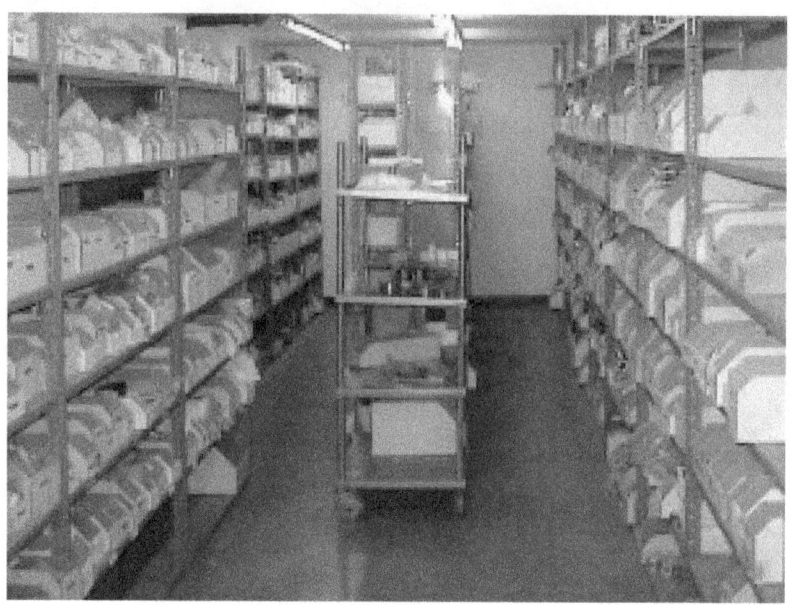

HIT THE LIGHTS

BOG'S A WRECK. At work, they have an arrangement where members of the Quality Department have to take turns giving a thirty minute lunchtime lecture to employees on a Quality related topic of their choice, and it's Bog's turn. He had no idea that this was part of the job and had a panic attack.

Ray's helping him work up a presentation using a variation of one of his roadside sermons on the hidden hazards of using *Common Sense*. Which doesn't make sense but Elly supposes someone like Bog could pull it off. Otherwise, he's doing better at work than she expected, she's surprised he's lasted this long; she just hope he doesn't get into trouble. He's become something of a renegade hero by running a successful bootleg office supply operation out of his cube.

There's an administrative assistant (they don't say "secretary" anymore) who has always been a bit of a problem. She was given the task of setting up and running the office supply stockroom and she did a fantastic job, it was the best equipped stockroom Elly's ever seen. The trouble is, she liked to keep it fully stocked and resented having her supplies depleted. She liked to see the shelves full. So her overall policy was that you couldn't take anything unless you *really* needed it and she developed approval procedures and forms to make sure you *really* needed whatever it was you wanted. She also kept track of what you got before and would typically ask questions like: "Why do you wanted a box of paperclips when you just got a box six months ago?" After a while, people tried to find other ways of getting what they wanted and often ended up bringing in their own supplies (paper, pens, staples and so forth) from home, but the overall problem remained. Bog soon discovered this situation and sized the opportunity. He used his P. O. (Purchase Order) allowance (employees in his category can spend a few dollars for job related expenses each month without any other approvals). His only problem was to disguise the purchases as Quality Department material. He pulled it off by adjusting his descriptions and by ordering the supplies from the non-typical stationary suppliers. He keeps the stuff in his file cabinet and freely gives it out after quietly letting it be known that he had extra supplies. It's not like he's selling it or anything, it's more along the lines of building up good will, also it's kind of a *Godfather* deal where the phrase "...some day I will ask you a favor..."

comes to mind. Anyway, he's making a name for himself.

Elly's making a bit of a name for herself too. She had her debut at *Loamers*. Louie and Black Ivy came to watch and Ruby came to fend off the drunks, but, being a Sunday afternoon, there wasn't much trouble. There weren't many customers either, but enough for Elly. They were well behaved and seemed to like the show. There's nothing like a little applause to get someone charged up. She only needed nine of her songs, the pace was slow and there weren't any encore calls. But, all-in-all, she feels that it well fairly well. Two people even asked for her autograph. She wishes Ray could have come, but he had to go up to Hanover for his contract preaching job with the Calvinites. (Their preacher is on a two week sabbatical up on the Gaspe peninsular.) He said it went okay but they cancelled his second Sunday session. Elly says hey must have been disappointed that she couldn't come.

MENSA MISFITS

BOG HAD A BUS LOAD OF BRAINS last Saturday. It was an exceptional group of fairly smart people called the *Carinas*. It's a worldwide private club with a chapter out of Concord. To be a member, all you have to do is take their IQ test and score above ninety percent of what they believe the worldwide average is, <u>but</u> no higher than ninety seven per cent. So, you have to be smart, but not *too* smart to be a member.

They rented the meeting room bus because the place they had been using, the old *Hemp Trader's Hall*, went smoke free. Since some of them smoke cigars and pipes, they wanted to find another place where they could feel relaxed and Bog's bus fit the bill. Since it was on the weekend, Bog was able to run the bus for the first time. He got his Commercial Drivers License (CDL) okay and had been practicing around the neighborhood. The only mishap was his own mailbox. He flattened it by not swinging wide enough as he drove out of his driveway and drove over it with the double rear wheel. He's better now but they're all still a little nervous.

During the Carinas' meeting, he planned to stay in the driver's seat to work on his employee Quality presentation for work. He and Louie had installed a sort of cloth shower curtain affair, to close the driver in the corner and give the illusion of privacy for the tenants. But, the Carinas invited him to sit with them as a guest. After conducting some routine club business, they broke out their own music, a case of champagne, plastic cups and just lounged around socializing. Two software engineers played cribbage while debating the value of Laplace transform algorithms. A physicist and a professor played dominoes as they tried to reconcile Einstein's theory of relativity against Kant's concept of space (where Kant says space only exists where it's filled up by something; but Einstein says it not only exists, it's a real thing that can, and does, get bent). Overall, the evening went well and they all had a fine time, including Bog. They've also reserved the bus for the second Saturday of each month for the next six months.

Ray says he ran into a chapter of them in Atlanta a few years ago. He says they're nice enough and quite affable but they're also somewhat solemn. He says, unlike most of us, they're smart enough to know how smart they're not. By requirement, they know the specific limit of their individual intellect, and it leaves them in a position where they're high enough to observe the truly intellectual world, but not quite tall enough to legitimately participate.

It seems to Elly that there's a club for most almost everyone; you see them advertised as you enter most any town: *Masons, Lions, Legionairs, Hibernians, Knights of Columbus, Elks, Odd Fellows*, and others. They've already acknowledged that the Ollie Khan Church is much like a club too, so Elly felt she's in no position to criticize.

They stopped advertising quite a while ago. Both Monday night sessions are full; they could add a third, but nobody's up for that. They've increased the requested donation to $20 to slow down the crowd but it hasn't had much effect.

Business has also picked up at the Inn. They've already started renting the four upstairs rooms in Orchard's house. The three downstairs rooms will be ready soon.

Elly's second Sunday playing at *Loamers* went well. Ray was able to come an watch this time. The club's manager recognized him (from her visit to Monday Night Church) and gave him a free Cajun corn beef sandwich. Bog came too. He was still going on about his meeting with the *Carinas*. The leader (or chairman) of the group tried to talk him into taking their test, but Bog wouldn't bite; he told them that he might try later if some of their smartness rubs off.

UNCOMMON SENSE

BOG PRESENTED his "Common Sense Hazards" lunch time lecture at work. Elly doubts if they'll ask him to do it again. He gave them a preview so that he could rehearse the presentation. Ray's to blame for most of it. He started with the dictionary's definition of *common sense*: "Sound but unsophisticated judgement of ordinary men" (it was an old, pre-politically correct edition). So, right off the bat, if someone tells you to "...just use a little common sense..." they're telling you that your problem is not complicated and within the expertise of "ordinary men;" but, Bog explained that some problems are more complicated than they appear and beyond the scope of common sense. For examples, he started with the obvious: If you saw a fire, common sense would suggest that you throw water on it. But of course that would be a bad move if it were an electrical or grease fire. Less obvious and in direct defiance of common sense: "If your coal stove's burning too hot, how do you cool it down?" Surprisingly, the correct method is to put *more* coal on the fire! (Elly didn't believe this but Louie said he was right. In fact, too much coal will actually put the fire out.) Thirdly (Black Ivy confirmed this): If you have an airplane and you want to be sure that other pilots see you, should you paint it *red* or *white*? You can guess what common sense would say, but the correct answer is *white,* because it reflects the most light. He went on with a few more cases like this, which made them think of their own examples. Ruby told them how *supply side* economics seem to contradict common sense. Louie got all wound up and told them about one of his customers who insisted that it was common sense that you can make a heating system work faster by turning the thermostat all the way to the top. He said she kept breaking the linkage on her car's temperature selector. When it was cold, she would jam it all the way to the right until the car eventually overheated, then she would slam it hard to the left side until it got cold and she would slam it back to hot and repeat the process during her whole trip. No matter how hard he tried, Louie couldn't convince her otherwise. Finally, he had to modify the levers of her linkage so that the max heat *position* would surreptitiously position the final (and hidden) control arm to the *mid*-range position, so she would slam it once to the far right where it would heat up to a comfortable, medium level and she would leave it alone.

Bog finished with a cartoon that he drew (with a Ray's help) that he put up on the overhead projector showing two professors in front of a large blackboard filled with a lengthy, complex calculus equation and one professor pointing to the board and shrugging to the other: "It's common sense!" The overall theme was that you need to resist the urge to jump to the common sense conclusion, at least not until you're sure of how deep the problem is or how things really work. Afterwards, they celebrated with some champagne that was left over from the Carina's meeting.

    Louie got drunk. He had another reason to celebrate; he got both of his Ukrainian girlfriends back. They reconciled (with each other) and asked him to take them back. He agreed and they're planning a trip to Quebec together next month. Elly thinks he should give a lecture on the merits (or hazards) of double dating, Franco-Asian style.

SHIFTY BUSINESS

SOME PEOPLE HAVE OFFERED TO BUY Black Ivy's sky printing business. They're looking for the whole package even her business telephone number. These people are working on a deal with the Vermont Highway Department to use the sky printing scheme for notifying motorists of road hazards and other traffic conditions. They also want all of her and Louie's design documentation. Black Ivy warned them about the competition but they already knew about the other plane and said Black Ivy's configuration was better for their application because they'll be printing the letters one above the other as they fly along the roadway. Black Ivy says, if they can settle on the details, she'll let it go. The main problem is that this will leave Black Ivy without a source of income, so she'll either have to get a job or another business.

Bog wants her to take over the *Cloud Nine Conference Haul* bus, but she's not interested. He's trying to focus more on his job after getting into a little trouble at the office. One of the Carinas, a wholesaler out of Laconia, gave him a deal on a case of industrial looking slippers.

Bog paid next to nothing for them. They're fairly ugly but very comfortable (he gave all of them a pair). To unload them, he took a bunch into work and sold them out of his cube as *Office Slippers*. He sold a few and was hoping to start a new trend but his boss found out and put a quick stop to it. The fact that he already put the boss in a bad mood didn't help. A few days earlier, Bog asked him how to apply for a *Golden Parachute*. Bog didn't really know what it meant; he thought it was some kind of special benefit but the boss just assumed he was being a trouble maker.

Since the high price of gasoline looks like trouble, Louie's looking for ways to revive his gas station. He's thinking of getting ready to support alternate fuels such as hydrogen, ethanol or bio-diesel. He says there's an interesting variation of bio-diesel that uses old vegetable oil. Some people are already using it. They collect used cooking oil from area restaurants and filter it. Once preheated, it can run in a diesel engine.

But you have to use regular diesel fuel to start the engine to preheat the vegetable oil, so you need a dual fuel tank and a valve to switch from one to the other. Ruby says he could get tons of used oil from all the fried seafood places over on the coast. Bog says he can see it now, "...This Grease-mobile gets thirty two miles a clam-fat gallon!"

Ray's getting more milage out of his Listening business. His drawing skills have improved enough that he's including a portrait with his house calls. As he sits with them, he sketches their caricature while they talk. At the end of the session, he leaves the drawing with them. He says that most of them like it and it makes him feel better, as though he's giving them something more than just his attention for their money. His work's not like those caricature artists that one sees at fairs or the beach, his drawings are just pen and ink and more stylized, like Elly's poster drawing for Loamers.

Her Sunday shows are going pretty well. The manager moved her to the late evening slot; she's calling her a "closer." She's also offering her a six month contract at five percent more a session than she's been getting. Bog said Elly should be sure not to ask for a *Golden Parachute*.

PHONE ARCADE

ELLY'S STUDIO COMPUTER IS TALKING TO HER. Louie's been working with her audio editing software again. This time it's speech. Bog and Black Ivy are in on it too. Between the three of them, he's created seven different people (by changing the voice pitch) who are acting as the characters in his phone-maze game. To create the maze, he bought a phone information directory software package: one of those annoying voice prompt message menu systems. It works like this:

You dial into the computer.

Black Ivy's normal voice answers: "Hello this is Wing's Aural Entertainment System, if you know what you're doing, press One to play, or press Five for instructions."

You press Five.

Black Ivy continues: "Your keypad is your control panel, press One to answer 'Yes,' or Seven to say 'No.' For maneuvering, press Four to go west, Two to go north, Six to go east and the Eight key to go south. To go up, press Three, and the Nine key to go down. For information in any location, press the Five key. To exit, hit Zero. To hear this again, press Five, if you're ready for action, press One or press Three to resume your last game."

You press One.

Black Ivy returns (Elly wonders how they talked her into this):

"You're facing northward and looking at the front door of your dead Uncle Walter's mansion. He's left it to you. But, your evil cousin, Malicia, tricked him into signing an alternate will, leaving the place to *her* instead of you. She's hidden it somewhere in the mansion. You have to find and destroy it before she returns and files it with the probate court. There's also a car behind you that says 'Perkins Property Appraisers' on the side. The door to the mansion is unlocked, do you wish to enter?"

You press One.

"You're in an ornate foyer. To the west is a parlor, to the north is a long, dark hall, beside it, there's a grand six foot wide flying staircase, to the east, is an entrance to a vast living or ballroom."

You press Two.

"You're in the middle of a long hall. To the north you can see the kitchen. To the west, there's a closed door. To the east, there's another closed door. To the south you can see the foyer."

You press Four.

A woman screams and you hear the door slam closed. Black Ivy gives you some advise: "You should knock before going into a washroom."

You press Two.

You hear Bog's voice: "Hello? I'm Pablo Perkins, we're appraising the property for Ms. Wort. Please don't get in the way."

Black Ivy's voice returns: "You're in the kitchen. To the west, you see a large dining room. To the north, a back door. To the east, a short hallway. To the south a long hall. Beside it, a closed door."

You press Nine.

You hear a door open and footsteps in a stairway. "There's a glowing furnace to the south; it's dark in all directions except to the north, where there's a stairway. Do you wish to turn on the light?"

You press One.

"There's a bright but brief flash of light and now it's dark again. During the flash, you think you saw someone scurry away from behind the furnace."

It goes on like this for quite a while. The player can move throughout the mansion and meet other people and find objects on the way. Louie says he's going to add more detail later. Elly thinks she'll press Zero.

WHO'S THAT KNOCKIN'

A DOOR-TO-DOOR SALESMAN CAME TO THE INN. It was an artist. A pleasant but musky looking middle aged man with a plaid shirt and a baseball hat that said *CAT*. He had a case of ledger sized acrylic paintings with one attached to the outside cover of his case. He knocked at the door (people are suppose to just come in and go to the desk). Ruby answered and he held up the case, chest high, presenting a painting of a girl chasing a horse in a field with Mount Monadnock in the background. He smiled and said: "Good day Ma'am, you have a lovely home here but it looks like it could use a little artwork."

Elly was surprised Ruby didn't chase him off; instead, she hesitated a moment then brought him in to sit in the lobby. As he entered, he removed his hat, and she nodded approvingly. Both Elly and Ruby were taken aback a bit. It's been decades since anyone's come to the door selling anything (Fuller Brush Men and Avon Ladies). He had about a dozen paintings, unframed on those thin canvas boards that you see in art supply section of some stores. One by one he passed them to Ruby and she passed them to Elly. They were all originals; not prints. They asked him about his door-to-door sales strategy. He said that galleries and art shows cost way too much and that this was a much more effective way to move the products, although a bit more risky with dogs and all. The price for each was two twenty. All of them were landscapes or cityscapes of various sorts but each showed at least one person in it, doing something. Ruby bought one with a dog laying on the ground beside a boy sleeping in a wooden wheelbarrow, next to a pile of split wood with the maul stuck in an unsplit log. The artist thanked them and gave her a ten dollar coupon towards having it framed at his sister in-law's shop up in Brattleboro. They hung it (without a frame) in the dining room suite of Orchard's house. Ruby said some of the other rooms could use a few paintings as well, but perhaps they'll look around at flea markets and yard sales.

All three of the downstairs rooms, as well as the bathroom, are finished and ready for occupants. Ray, Louie and Bog finished the covered walkway between the two buildings, as well as the corrected handicap ramp. They're still waiting for the inspector to return.
Meanwhile, Bog and his bus hosted the *Carinas* for the second time. More cigars and champagne, but, this time, they took advantage of his

mobility and held their meeting in the afternoon up at Lake Sunapee. One of the members, the owner of a Panoz (some kind of American sports car) dealership, has a boat  there and took everyone for a tour of the lake, eight at a time including Bog. Another member is the Sales Manager of a Volvo dealership. Bog asked her, now that Ford owns them will you finally be able to get one of those fancy Volvo wagons with imitation wood paneling on the side. Bog thought he was being funny but, being a Carina, she didn't laugh. Instead, she seemed to be trying to determine the implications of the possibility. It's hard to be funny when the jokes get analyzed. She also analyzed Bog. She said he might make a good salesman and they need at least one more. She encouraged him to come in and fill out an application.

    Bog later talked to Ruby about career possibilities. She said he should be an artist; she says they're held to a lower moral standard and he could use the extra leeway.

HASTY COMPOST POWER

Black Ivy's FINALIZING THE SALE OF HER PLANE and sky printing business. They've settled on a price and she's agreed to sign a document saying she won't replicate the business or otherwise compete with them for five years. Now, she has to find something else to do and has no plans to get another plane. But, she'd like to use the money to get another business going. Bog thinks they could convert her airstrip (behind their house) to an apple orchard or a long, thin alpaca farm. Carla (the Cuban cowgirl) wants her to raise horses and have pony rides. But Black Ivy's neither a farmer nor a rancher. Ruby thinks you can probably make out okay if you can find a way to sell *time*. That is, give people in a hurry quick service for whatever they need so they won't be late getting to whatever place or event they're rushing off to. She says people seem to like whatever's fast: fast-food, fast-photos, fast-pass toll booths, etc. Bog says he wishes that he could get a fast haircut, he also wishes they had more express checkout lanes in the grocery store.

Black Ivy asked Louie if he thought someone could succeed by selling fast-gas, that is, a full service setup with attendants standing by so customers could stay in their car and get their gas pumped by someone else, like the old days but quicker. Louie said the key to selling gasoline is volume, and the cost of attendants would force you to sell the gas too high, killing the volume. You couldn't compete. But Black Ivy thinks Ruby's on to something with her fast service strategy and that you might be able to compete with *time*; some people are always in an awful hurry and they would probably pay a premium for speed. It's just a matter if *enough* people would. She thought you could also make it fast by having no choices: offer only regular gas and only fill-ups on a debit card or a fixed dollar amount for cash. No credit cards, unless you could speed up or eliminate the signature process. A car would pull in. The moment they stopped and popped their gas lid lever, an attendant would immediately start filling the tank. She wondered if you could get the pumps to pump faster. Louie didn't think so.

Black Ivy was also interested in his earlier alternate fuels idea. He says, in the long run, fuel cells burning hydrogen will have the best chance of success, but they're several years away from getting the technology worked out. Bio diesel has a bit of a future but it's sort of a niche market right now that may or may not grow. But, in the short run, ethanol is the most promising. He says the technology's already here and they're making it out of corn right now but they're also working on ways to make it from scrap organic material. Black Ivy says fast gas with ethanol on the side might be worth a try. Bog said she should lease Louie's station and give it a try. But Louie said the location's no good for the volume she'd need. It would have to be in a high traffic location with a lot of people in a hurry.

Bog was still thinking about making bio-diesel from organic scrap. He wondered if they could make it from tobacco. He says you could also have a recycling program, where people would bring in their old corn cobs and coffee grinds and you could give them credits for their ethanol purchase. Trash for gas.

GET YOUR EYES ON THE ROAD

THERE'S A CAMCORDER BOLTED TO THE HOOD of Louie's car. Front and center, like the amber Indian head on the nose of a '53 Pontiac. These days, he's driving an old State Police cruiser. It's a brown and green Ford Crown Victoria with a big push bar, little hub caps and lurking spot lights, so it's already a fairly intimidating rig to begin with.

The camcorder is part of a scheme to raise money to develop his Telephone Arcade project. He's using it to produce local travel video DVDs by recording an up-front view of road trips from one city to another. Elly thought he'd want to edit them down, but no, they're full length, the entire boring trip; mile by mile, wide angle. The only enhancement he's making, is having Black Ivy record a voice-over narration at the beginning and at some of the key points or tricky intersections along the way. For the rest of the track, he has soft music in the background. He records the trips early on Sunday mornings then works with Black Ivy on the sound track during the week. So far, they've done: *Keene to Concord* and *Boston to Brattleboro*. Next, are other destinations from Boston, such as Newburyport, Lawrence, Worcester, Providence, and the Cape. Elly didn't think they would be very entertaining but he says they're not for entertainment, they're for directions. For instance, people planning to travel to one of these places would buy a DVD and preview the trip to see what they're getting into. Or, if you've got relatives flying in from out of state, you'd send them the one of these videos of the trip to your area, along with your final directions.

  Ray says Louie could produce a cross-country trip with a series of city to city videos. Ruby says he should do a foliage tour in mid-October, through the mountains. She said he could also work out a deal with the *destination* businesses, like the Louden race track, Foxwoods Casino, and the White Mountain ski resorts. She's already commissioned him to record the trip from the Manchester airport to the Inn. She says she'll send them to customers that have made reservations. At the end of the video, they'll have a shot of Ruby and Elly greeting them at the door. Bog wants Black Ivy to try the same thing from the air and put a camera on the landing gear of her next plane and produce aerial tour videos of New England. Black Ivy says it's already been done.

  She's more focused on finding a filling station for sale that she can convert to the "Fast Gas" operation that they were talking about last week. She seems to be serious and is already talking with sign and lighting companies, as well as petroleum wholesalers. She's not planning to go with any one brand. Rather, she'll get the gas from whomever gives her the best deal at the time, and sell it under her own name: "Ivy" in big red letters on a white background. She's also still planning on having just one grade. Ruby warned that Getty tried the same thing with just *high test* but the scheme didn't seem to last. Black Ivy thinks *89 octane* is the right compromise, since it's close enough to regular, but "a little bit better" to help justify the higher price. Again, the emphasis will be on fast service. She wasn't going to sell anything else, but while people are sitting in their driver's seat, waiting for their fill-up, she could have them look at a rack of travel related items for sale, like snacks, maps and Louie's traveling DVDs.

NOW HE'S GONE TOO FAR

THE FAST TALKING WOMAN FINALLY CAUGHT up to Ray. She had been on his waiting list for quite a while and some of his regulars have stopped calling him, so her turn came up. She spent the full hour with him complaining about her friends and relatives. She wants Ray to agree with her point of view, so it's a little tricky for him to be understanding without participating. He misses the sober women. Things seemed to begin tapering off with them when he started doing those pen and ink caricatures. Although most of the women seemed to like them, it was as though the transaction was completed or business was finished when he gave it to them; after all, why would anyone want more than one? So, he's stopped doing the drawings but he's still seeing the hollow woman and taking lessons.

On the bright side, the *Calvinites* called him back. Once again, they needed a substitute minister as their's is held up in a Canadian jail and will be stuck there for a while. Some trouble with Argentinian oil men, a stolen Bentley and drugs. Since she's working the evening shift now, Elly was able to go with him for the Sunday afternoon service and play (they've got a real organ). They borrowed Ruby's Pontiac and drove up. It was about an hour north, in the middle of nowhere. Their church was a converted barn with a tall silo that seemed to be serving as a sort of blunt steeple.

They wanted Ray to wear the minister's hat; kind of a black top hat without a brim, but he wouldn't. Otherwise, he used the same routine as at home, so it works out to be sort of a rehearsal for Monday Night Church. Except, the Calvins just sit there with thin lips held tight, so there's not much fooling around and no *question and answer* session. Elly doesn't know why they called Ray back, they don't seem to like him. Then again, she thinks they're a sour bunch who probably don't like anybody. They were talking about it on the way back, Ray said it might be the typical cult condition where the members feel that they're the *chosen ones* (the *only* ones), and having their chosen leader fall from grace might tarnish the whole premise of their divine connection. Ray's already agreed to a few weeks there but Elly wishes there was a way to get out of it. Her first impulse was to have Bog to substitute for Ray next week, just to shake them up.

A few days ago, he was at the Inn while Ruby was fretting about all the troubles caused by the hurricanes, tsunamis and terrorists and said: "Why does God let these awful things happen?"

Bog straightens up, thinks for a moment: "Maybe He's just being a big stinker."

"What!" snaps Ruby, with her eyebrows pinched together.

Calmly, and with his reflective face on, Bog continues: "You hear that 'God is *good*' but says *who*, how do they *know*, and what if He *isn't*?"

"What!"

"Suppose He's a *bad* guy who just happens to have all this power. Why do we assume He's *good*?" Usually Elly can tell when Bog's just trying to stir her up, but this time she couldn't be sure. He could have kept Ruby going, but he just left it hanging and wandered home without saying much else.

Ruby was more depressed than mad and says: "He's bought a ticket straight to Hell!" Elly thought they should send him to Canada wearing a black, brimless top hat.

RING IN THE HAT

RAY AND ELLY HAD ANOTHER SUNDAY with the Calvinites. It went a little better than last week, some of them even smiled. One couple talked to them afterwards, telling them how everyone's despondent over their convicted minister's questionable character. But, they seem to be warming up to Ray, and they keep trying to get him to wear that stupid hat. Once again, he declined. Later, he said the religious propensity for special hats is very curious, what with the Greek's black chimney pots, the Catholics' pointy miters, and the wide array of Jewish kippots; he's not sure what drives it. Elly guesses it's like any uniform; just a way to be identified. The next day, she was telling Ruby about the hat while Bog was over. She should have known better. He perks up and says that they should come up with an official hat for the Ollie Khan

Church. Says it'll make them more legitimate.

"Perhaps berets," he goes on. "Black ones for the men, red for the women and a white one for Ray."

"What about the kids?" said Elly, goading him on.

"None for the kids!" he said quickly. "They'll have to wait until they're 21, then we'll have a special ceremony with candles and songs where they get 'crowned' as official *Ollies"* (It never occurred to her that they'd be called *Ollies*.) "It'll be a big deal." he went on, "other kids will want to join, just so they can get an official hat." He paused a moment, "We'll have to come up with some way to make them unique to prevent counterfeit versions; something in the brim perhaps or maybe tall pointy ones that wiggle when you nod your head."

"I'm not wearing any damn hat!" growled Ruby.

Well, Elly decided she's not wearing any hat either, although she always thought the parading Shriners looked happy wearing their silly little flat-top fezzes and tassels. Maybe it makes you feel good.

In spite of happy hats, Ruby's been in a pretty good mood. Louie produced the DVD she asked for, showing the road trip from the Manchester airport to the Inn. He made fifty copies for her and she's already mailed out a few to some of her customers. Elly got a little car sick watching it. Louie produced them just before his trip to Quebec. He and his Ukrainian girlfriends drove up in his old police cruiser. They stayed at the Hotel Frontenac, and went whale watching on the St. Lawrence River near Baie St. Paul. He also recorded the whole trip (there and back) with his hood mounted camcorder and had a bit of explaining to do at Customs. Instead of Black Ivy, he had the Ukrainians do the voice-over narration.

Back home, Black Ivy's charging full steam ahead on her *Fast Gas* station idea, she's even got a business plan worked out that shows her being profitable in twenty four months. There are two properties that she's looking into: old garages, that have been out-classed by the new, multi-pump stations.

Meanwhile, Bog's found a way to keep Carla busy. He convinced her that, to be a famous kid, you have to have a good catch phrase, like: "Leapin' Lizards," "Good Grief," or "Great Horney Toads!" She bought in to it and is trying to come up with her own. She's already learned the value of alliteration and has come up with: "Jumpin' Jackals," "Holy Hyenas" and "Miserable Monkey Muffins." She goes around reciting these phrases while wearing her special red Bolivian shepherd's hat. No fame yet but she looks impressive and she's feeling proud. Elly thinks that maybe she'd like a red Ollie beret after all.

FRAGILE FOOTING

THERE'S A LITTLE BOY PEEING IN THE FRONT YARD of the church. He's about two and a half feet tall and made of cement. It's part of Bog's *wishing well* fountain design.

To keep the fountain interesting and to encourage donations, he changes the set-up and fixtures from time to time, but now he's caused a little controversy. To make it worse, he also has a little eighteen inch waterwheel in the fountain pool with a battery powered motor so that it turns in the water. He has it in front of the boy and has him (with his pump running) aimed at the wheel so that it looks like the boy's stream is making the wheel turn. The kids laugh and it makes them happy, but not the parents. Some have begun to use the question and answer cards to lodge their complaints.

The kids also use the cards, but to submit requests, either for favorite songs or stories. Some of them wanted to hear more about the *Polliwog Princess* so Ray came up with a new episode where the princess gets a job as a mannequin and models children's clothing in department stores. She stands perfectly still for up to two minutes beside real mannequins and only moves, or repositions herself, when no one's looking; unless there's a little boy shopping with his mother.

If the boy is looking at her while the mother isn't, the princess sticks out her tongue at him, or if he isn't looking, she reaches out and pinches his ear. In either case, the boy would yell and tell his mother, who doesn't believe him and ends up dragging him off by the wrist. You never know if there's suppose to be a point or a lesson in these stories. Elly can't tell.

Nevertheless, she thinks Monday Night Church is going pretty well. The first session has evolved into the family portion, with a lot of kids, while the second show has become an adults only affair. So the latter session is similar, but without the Polliwog Princess, and the tone gets more serious and a little saucier. A few people from the first show stay for the second. The crowd is fairly regular and the revenue from the donation jug is reasonably dependable. The man with the white belt is still coming and he's been talking to the weird couple (the ones with hair horns and body ornaments) about something. The college kids keep showing up, taking notes and buying the DVDs. Ruby helps Bog with the books and says they've got a pretty solid business going. But, she adds that the whole operation is very fragile because it all depends on Ray, and it could fall apart if any thing happened to him. She says they should work out a back-up plan and asked Elly if she's picked up any of his preaching skills along the way.

Elly doesn't feel that she has, but she thinks it's odd that it would come up now because Ray's been a bit moody lately. He says he's all right but she knows he isn't. Something's bothering him. You'd think it'd be the sour faced Calvinites getting him down, but she doesn't think so. The Sunday sessions up there seem like one of the high points of his week. He's usually smiling afterwards. She called his brother, Ralph, to see if he knew anything. He said not to worry. He says Ray runs into philosophical conflicts from time to time when he's developing sermons, but he usually gets over it in a week or two. Elly thinks a new statue for the fountain would cheer him up.

GHOSTLY GAS

BLACK IVY BOUGHT A HAUNTED GAS STATION. That is, she's in the process, with a signed purchase and sales agreement which is dependent on (among other things) an examination of the soil (to make sure the tanks haven't leaked). It's an old Texaco station that's been closed for over a year, with two bays and one pumping island. It would be a fairly normal property except for the stories of ghost sightings. It used to have a pit in one of the bays and one morning, years ago, a mechanic who was working late under an old Studebaker, was found the next morning in the bottom of the pit, dead. They don't know what happened to him but more than one person claims they've seen him since, roaming around inside the station. They usually see him just out of the corner of their eye. Oddly, the realtor was required to disclose the reports of these sightings. Ruby believes it but says he (the ghost) is probably harmless. Carla's nervous but trying to be brave and says they should make friends with him. Normally, Elly would expect Bog to come up with an odd twist on the whole situation to try to be funny or make them nervous, but he's remaining quiet and seems to be uncomfortable with the idea. Black Ivy could care less.

Elly's never gone along with these stories, but it does make her wonder. She gets nervous whenever she has to clean up in Orchard's house alone. It's just that she hears about these things so much, she wonders if there might be something to it. She asked Ray, (who's still in a slump), he says no one can be sure because we don't know what we don't know but, with what we do know, there's no rationale or metaphysic that supports the idea. He says that most of the time, people who see ghosts are the same people who *expect* to see ghosts. He says this also applies to the fringe religions and the UFO enthusiasts. For once, Ray made her feel better, and she guesses she can think of a lot of people who are ready to start seeing things. The first people who come to mind, are the Calvenites. They seem like just the sort of folks who would be prone to visions, but she won't get a chance to find out.

Once again, they've cut Ray's contract short and sent him packing. At first, Elly thought they must have found someone else who's willing to wear their silly minister's hat, but it turns out that it's the silly minister himself. He got out of the Canadian jail early and he wasn't too happy that Ray had taken his place. It's hard to tell if it bothers Ray, since he's already in a rut.

Ruby's noticed but doesn't offer much sympathy. She's been nagging him to run the church in a more conventional manner, with prayers and sermons that are more religious. She says it should be in his job description. Ray wasn't very agreeable but he did go along with her next idea, where she said they should have *guest preachers* once in a while. Ray said he could recommend some from the agency he works with but reminded her that they'd have to pay them.

Since it involves spending money, they thought they should have a Church business meeting to discuss and vote on it. Ruby told Bog and he agreed to set one up. That'll give him something to do to keep his mind off the garage ghost.

THE MEETING WILL COME TO CHAOS

THEY HELD THEIR FIRST CHURCH BUSINESS MEETING, with Bog in charge. Before the meeting, he read up on Orchard's charter for the Church to see what the rules were and he went to the library to look at *Robert's Rules of Order* to see how to run the meeting. He did a fairly decent job, up to a point.

They met in the old kitchen of Orchard's house. Bog's first order of business, was to appoint a Church Clerk (to record the attendance and take the minutes). Ruby quickly volunteered and was unanimously elected. Next, Bog had Black Ivy move to set up a regular monthly meeting. They all thought it wasn't such a bad idea and voted okay. Among Orchard's bylaws, Bog found a requirement for a two thirds majority in order to approve any financial transactions (other than normal operating expenses). In their current case, that means they'll need four votes to spend any money. The whole point of this was to see about hiring guest ministers and Ruby got impatient and wondered why Bog wasn't getting to the main issue. Bog said somebody had to make the motion. Ruby made the motion. Elly started to second it. but Bog moved right on to the discussion phase before she could.

"What about my second!?" hollers Ruby.

Bog said it's not required. He said the reason for requiring a second is to prevent some troublemaker from making frivolous motions and disrupting meetings, but *Roberts* says its not necessary in small boards.

"The only troublemaker here, is the one running the meeting!"

With no further trouble making, they talked about the benefits, complications and cost of having guest ministers. Bog eventually called for the vote. Ruby, Ray and Elly were for it, the rest were not, so it didn't carry. Elly worried that this business of voting may eventually cause some hard feelings in the group. Bog was worried about another problem, he said that with just the six of them, the chance of a tie (in votes where the two thirds weren't required) is going to be a problem and perhaps they should find another member to replace Orchard.

They started to kick around ideas on who they'd recruit. Louie offered up his girlfriends (but they'd still be stuck with an even number and you couldn't have one without the other). Bog knew a Carina that might be interested. Ruby said we don't need any *smart asses*. Ray suggested the hollow woman (Martha Whitman). They couldn't think of anyone else so they agreed to have Ray talk to her about it. After that, they talked about the general operation.

Bog thought they should get a bigger chapel so that they could handle the full crowd and go back to the single sessions. Ruby said they should leave it the way it is and not let a little success go to their heads. Ray agreed with Ruby and said he liked the size of the meetings and variety of the dual sessions. Black Ivy said they should come up with some sort of entrance criteria and "find a way to keep those darn college kids from coming."

"There's nothing wrong with those kids," said Ruby. "It's that nasty girl with the horns in her hair that we got to get rid of!"

"If you're gonna get rid of anyone," continued Black Ivy, "it should be that guy in the white belt!" They all agreed that they could get along without *white belt*. Except for Ray; he kept quite and just listened. Overall, they got nothing done and Bog eventually adjourned the meeting.

TAKE THIS WOMAN

A NICE WEDDING IN THE CHAPEL is what Ruby and Elly had been hoping for, instead, they're getting the opposite. For the past few weeks, Ray's been acting as sort of a marriage counselor for the daughter of one of his lady listening customers. The woman was hoping that Ray would be able to straighten things out and help them stay together. He's listened, separately, to both the girl and her husband; neither one wants to work it out and they both want to split-up, but surprisingly, they want to do it on good, or at least civil, terms. Ray, to the mother's dismay, eventually agreed that, in their case, it would best to end the relationship. But, somehow, the girl feels that since a ceremony got them into this, another ceremony should get them out, and this persuasive girl has talked Ray into having a *divorce* ceremony at the church; the boy doesn't like the idea, but he's willing to go along with it; "...whatever it takes," he says.

The unhappy event is scheduled for this Friday evening (after work). The girl's father is dead, so Louie is going to stand in for him and *take her back.* There's no maid of honor, no reception and no cake. Elly thinks it's stupid. Ruby thinks that Ray overstepped his authority. It's definitely something they should have voted on.

On a happier note, he's convinced Martha the hollow woman to join the Church fellowship (to be the seventh voter). But first, she wanted to meet with them. Ray took her to Bog and Black Ivy's for a visit. Bog explained the church's history, purpose and structure. Then, Ray brought her to the Inn for a talk with Ruby and Elly. But of course, the woman doesn't talk, (to them anyway). Rather, Ray moderates and she listens. Elly guesses it went well, but it's hard to tell. She shook their hands and almost smiled.

After Ray brought her home, the six of them had another kitchen business meeting and took a vote. They were all for it, except Black Ivy. She thinks the woman might be evil and voted no. Elly thought this would put Bog on the spot, but it didn't seem to affect him. He said: "five to one; motion carried," and instructed the scowling clerk, Ruby, to have the woman sign the membership form (the same form that Orchard had them sign).

In spite of the hollow woman, Black Ivy's excited. She signed and passed the papers for the haunted gas station, even though the soil test showed some leaking. She could have gotten out of the deal, but the owner agreed to lower the price to offset the reconstruction costs. They have to replace the tanks and the soil around them with clean gravel. Black Ivy was going to replace the tanks anyway and had already figured that part of it into her business plan. She's registered her business name: "Ivy89" and is shopping for a sign maker, a lighting contractor, new gas pumps and gasoline wholesalers. As the name implies, she'll be selling exclusively *89octane*, which she hopes will simplify the whole operation. Bog's pretty excited too and wants to have a celebration at the Inn. He likes parties. On the television shows about remodeling or buying houses, he always hears the owners say that they "...love to entertain." Well, he says he loves *to be* entertained. He also said they should have a *divorce shower* for the poor girl who wants to get unmarried; with dried flowers and black balloons. Carla wondered what would be the opposite of a honeymoon.

NOT *TOO* SMART

R AY'S IN MUCH BETTER SPIRTS but Bog's gone moody. The Friday night divorce ceremony went okay. Since it seemed like something of an historic event, they all attended. Ruby and Elly sang an opening song: a modified version of Betsy Banks' *Go Now*. Ray gave a short and sober but unexpectedly comforting talk. Their lawyer was there (one lawyer representing both of them) and had them sign some papers. Ray had Bog stand in for the Best Man and retrieve the rings. With papers signed and rings removed, Ray pronounced the marriage dissolved. No kissing, Ray just said: "shake hands and go in peace." They shook hands. Louie stood in for the father and escorted the girl out of the church. Once she drove off with her mother, Bog walked the boy out and he drove off alone. No one was happy but there was a sense of relief in the air. It also seems to have lifted the cloud off of Ray and he's definitely out of his slump. The rest of them are still feeling a little glum. But it's not the *anti-wedding* that's made Bog moody. First it was the *Carinas*, then it was Ray.

Bog still hosts the *Carinas* once a month. Each time he takes them in his *Cloud Nine Conference Haul* bus, they invite him to join the social part of the meeting and the chairman always tries to get Bog to take their entrance exam, to see if his intelligence is in the top ninety percent (but no higher than ninety seven percent) of the world's average (smart but not *too* smart). Bog finally agreed. The exam's not like a test in school; rather, it's an IQ test where the examiner (the *Carinas'* Admissions Secretary) interviews you and verbally asks you questions or shows you a set of pictures, and you verbally respond or point at the right one. The exam was extensive and amazingly, Bog passed! He's no genius, but he's in the top ninety percent (just barely) and officially classified as having a "superior" intellect. Ruby doesn't believe it and thinks the *Carinas'* are looking to get a free conference room rental. Elly thought he'd be thrilled but he seems troubled by it. He says he doesn't know what to make of it because he doesn't feel very smart and says he's actually a little depressed because it's somewhat unsettling to know that most everyone else *isn't* as smart as you are (he assumed most people were smarter). He also feels that he should be taking life more seriously now and not acting as silly as he has been. (They all think Bog's silly but Elly was surprised to here *him* say so.) Anyway, he's eligible to join the *Carinas* and they want him to sign up, but he wasn't sure if he should. He asked Ray for his advice. Ray's usually open minded, but, without even thinking it over, he quickly advised Bog *not* to. Instead, and out of the blue, he told Bog that he should be thinking about marrying Black Ivy. Usually Elly thinks she can predict how Ray's going to react to a situation, but then he says something like this and pulls the rug out from under her. Of course, Ruby's been saying that for years and feels it would be good for both Bog and Black Ivy and it would set a better example for Carla. She also says, if Ray's the one to marry them, he might be able to redeem himself, after his part in Friday's sorry ceremony.

SENIOR THUG

THEY MOVED ELLY TO FRIDAY EVENINGS at *Loamer's*. The crowd's completely different and definitely rougher. Young men in dungarees and blue collared women winding down and drinking up after a hard week's work. She's glad Ray comes with her and sits near the stage, because they often get rowdy and start bumping each other around. Last Friday, in the middle of a four man shoving match, was an older man, perhaps in his seventies. He was drinking and shoving the younger men, just like he was one of them. He had a leather jacket, a wrinkled bald head, stringy gray sideburns and seemed to be looking for a fight. Ray interceded and had the man sit with him. The wrinkled man was reluctant at first, but eventually calmed down and lost his edge and seemed to be transformed, as though he moved from one world into another. Ray talked to him for quite a while, or mostly just listened. It turns out that he's living hard on purpose. He doesn't want to grow old and end up in a nursing home. Not exactly a death wish, but he's hoping to go out quickly with a bang. It's not that he looks for overtly dangerous activities (sky diving and such), he's just living hard and hoping for the best. The trouble is, he's been at it for over ten years without making much progress, other than a lot of bumps and bruises. He's been trying to think of ways to improve his odds. Ray was careful not to offer any suggestions.

On his way out at the end of Elly's set, one of the younger men, that he had been scuffling with earlier, elbowed him in the side as he walked by. Without hesitation, the old man lunged at the other with fists flying, knocking the younger man off his chair and on to the floor. The old man leaped on top of him with his old elbows swinging. Other men jumped and tables toppled. A confusing fight with several men involved went on for at least five minutes. The police arrived and dragged the old man and two others off. On his way through the door, under the grip of a large officer, the old man turned back and under a smudged bloody nose, gave Ray a smile and an "oh what the heck" wave goodbye.

Elly started to worry about *her* pending old age and wonder who'll end up taking care of her if she can't. Ruby's thought about it too and says the whole prospect makes her mad. Says she'll shoot anyone that tries to put her in a home. Ray says the old man's real problem is that he's alone.

At least none of them, at the moment, are alone. Louie was alone for a while and not too happy about it so they hope he can hang on to at least one of his girlfriends. They also hope that Bog can hold on to Black Ivy and they'd feel better if he'd follow up on Ray's suggestion and marry her. Of course, she might not go for it. She's already refused to marry Carla's father. Anyway, all of her attention is focused on the new gas station. It's coming together pretty well; the tanks and surrounding gravel are being replaced. The signs, lighting and pump island canopy are next. She'll run the station herself and Louie will help her out for the first few weeks but she's also advertising for help and plans to hire two people. She should be ready for business in a month or so.

WAG THE BOG

RAY'S GOT JOB. Another "fill in" preaching position, this time for the "Willow Apostate Group" over the river in Vermont. According to Ray, they're more of a lost religion, with parishioners made up of former members from various churches (Jews, Catholics, assorted Protestants and even a few Muslims) who are looking for something else, but they haven't found it yet. They examine every belief and take a critical view of it, weeding out all that they believe is wrong, wicked or wacky and then see what's left. They're at a point where they've gone through all the major religions, now they're looking for more obscure ideas to consider. Ray says that's where he comes in.

Elly doesn't know what that means and she don't like the sound of it. Ray says it's an intriguing endeavor. He says if you first discount the Jewish claims of divinity, then you also have to discount the Christians and Muslims along with them (since they share the same foundation). That mostly leaves just the Taoists, Hindus and Buddhists, and, of course (he says) Buddhism is more of a philosophy than a religion, so there's not much left, leaving you to wonder what the

Willows are thinking.

Well, she don't know what to think about it and she's not sure if she wants any Apostates discounting them. They heard about their Ollie Khan outfit from Bog when they rented his conference room bus for one of their off-site meetings. They were very curious and asked him a lot of questions about the Church and he told them what he could but they want to hear more from the resident minister. Bog told them about Ray and his contract preaching business. They were also interested in his probable exposure to other obscure churches (Bog told them about the Calvinites), so they've hired Ray for their weekly evening services (or club meeting) a week from Wednesday (they intentionally avoid Sundays and Saturdays). Ray says it'll be mostly a question and answer session but he wants her to come along with him anyway. Elly's not sure if she's mad at Bog or not.

But it's hard to be mad at him. He's been a little down in the dumps while trying to cope with his new found intellect. Carla keeps trying to get him to solve her Rubik's Cube and check her math homework. Ray's trying to steer him toward philosophical subjects, like epistemology, ethics and metaphysics. Bog wasn't interested; said that one of the grumpier Carinas already told him that these arguments loose much of their relevance if you suppose that humans never showed up. That is, if apes and monkeys were the best evolution could come up with, your Gospels, Discourses and Critiques of Reason would be just be wisps of ideas left blowing in the wind lifting no one.

Ruby still doesn't buy any of it and wants him to prove he's smart by coming up with a solution for the war on terror. Elly expected Bog to come up with some weird idea; instead he just said there'll be no winning it, he says it's like the war on poverty; you can make improvements but there'll be no end to the source of the problem. It was very unlike him and it seemed as though he had already been thinking about it. Nevertheless, Ruby's sure his IQ test was a hoax and suspects those Carinas are up to something. But Elly guesses she believes it. She was afraid he would try to act like a *know it all* and get preachy by trying to give them advice or his opinions on everything, but he hasn't.

Black Ivy, who's pretty smart herself, confided in Elly that Bog's always been semi-smart; she says half of him is fairly intelligent and the other half is less so. The trouble is, the dumber half is much quicker. Any hasty judgements or decisions, are usually trouble, but if he takes his time, he sees the deeper realities of issues and does all right. So Black Ivy's careful not to rush him to any big decisions. But the Carinas' have left him a bit discouraged. When he declined their invitation to join the club, they were disappointed and later cancelled their monthly conference bus booking, having rented another hall. Perhaps the Willows will become regular customers instead.

IVY 89

FAST GAS

R ISING HIGH IS BLACK IVY'S NEW SIGN, with large slanted red letters on a white, back-lit rectangle. Underneath it on a smaller, separate sign, more slanted letters say *"FAST GAS,"* but with "hites" behind them (those little horizontal lines that cartoonists use to show motion). Everything seems to be coming together pretty well, but Black Ivy's nervous; she's got all her money and a big loan tied up in the project and says she'll be in trouble if it doesn't fly. Nevertheless, the new tanks are in and covered with new cement and the rest of the area is newly paved. The gas pumps are mounted; their electronic connections are next. The frame for the pump station roof is up and the outside lighting is being installed. She's gone a bit overboard with the lights and will have nearly twice as many as you'd expect. She's also hired two workers, one's a twenty year old college girl who's studying economics at Keene State and has also been a cashier at the grocery store. The other's an old guy; a former fast food manager in his late sixties (who's just looking for something to do with his time). They'll both be wearing uniforms: red chinos, white shirts, red bow ties (clip on), red and white checkered hats and black shoes. Elly thought she knew who's idea it was, but Bog had no part in it. It's all Black Ivy's plan. Elly thinks she's trying to revive the earlier gas station service days; that's probably why she's hired the old guy; not many people would remember the real *full service* concept. Of course it's not going to be real full service, just someone to pump the gas for you. But Black Ivy's gambling that, along with fast service, being able to sit in your car will be enough. The attendants will be in a booth right at the pump island, so customers will know that they don't have to wait for someone to come out the garage and walk over to the car. It'll be a one direction operation and you will pull up to either the left or right side of the center pumps, depending if your car has a right or left side fill. As soon as you stop and release your gas cap cover, one of the attendants will immediately start filling your tank (since there's only one grade of gas there's no need to wait for the customer to make a choice), at the same time, the other attendant asks the driver how much they want by saying "Will that be a *fill up* Madam/Sir?" The second attendant will then present the portable card reader to the customer for them to scan in their debit or credit card, just like a grocery store. Unless they're paying with cash. When they open next week, Black Ivy will work the first shift with the old man, then Louie and the college girl will handle the second half of the day.

Apart from all the new construction, there's still the original building. Black Ivy's letting Louie use the two bays to sell used cars. The garage doors are glass, so he can have two cars well lit and on display but out of the weather. The little office will be a gift shop (for people who aren't in a rush) where they'll sell the trinkets that Bog's made over the years. Also, at the pumps, they'll sell maps, snacks and Louie's traveling DVDs. Black Ivy's hired the people who bought her plane to display an ad for her in the skies. Elly hopes it works.

GLAD WAGS AND NO SELF SERVICE

RAY AND ELLY HAD THEIR MEETING with the *Willow Apostate Group*. She expected them to be a glum and gloomy bunch. Instead, they were just a group of goofs. They met in a hall they rent above the shops downtown. They had an open bar and the meeting seemed like a combination between a Senate hearing and a New year's Eve party, with a lot of questions, laughing and clowning around. She and Ray sat at a table with microphones (not for speakers, but for recording). The members, about thirty or forty of them, sat in the audience drinking, socializing with each other and interrogating them. They had to repeat the questions for the recording. But the Apostates often debated among themselves, so Elly didn't think that got recorded.

She gave them the history of the original Ollie Khan Revival Church and described a typical service. Ray picked up the story from the point where Orchard got it going again, mainly for tax purposes. Beyond that, they were very interested in Ray's line of work and the different religions he's run across. He talked about more than just the Calvinites. It turns out there's an endless array of fringe religions that he's run across. Mostly home grown Christian variations. Ray says it all stems from conflicting interpretations of the Bible. He says the Catholics were smart to keep it out of the hands of the general public for as long as they did. They talked about how you don't seem to have this sort of problem in other main religions like Budism or Islam, perhaps the Koran is less ambiguous or the Muslims are not as prone to personal interpretation. Nobody knew if the Hindus had any splinter groups. They talked with Ray and among themselves about these and other religions, focusing on how they got started. Usually it's some opinionated and charismatic visionary with leadership ability at the root of all of them. The real mystery, they say, is where all these people who are ready to follow a new leader come from and how do they become so easily converted. Elly didn't know about conversion but she guessed the meeting went well; the Willows want them to come back in a few weeks.

Meanwhile, Black Ivy is looking for converts. She had her grand opening yesterday. Bog was there helping out. He wore short stilts (the kind dry wall workers wear), long striped pants and an Uncle Sam hat. He walked up and down the side of the road in front of the station waving at people with a yellow flag. Elly imagined he scared some away but several others came in. There was some confusion about the full service arrangement as many drivers started to get out of their cars to pump their own gas. Some of the younger drivers didn't even understand the concept. Black Ivy and Howard (the old guy she hired) had to work fast to keep people in their cars. They took turns with one waiting on the customers while the other pumped the gas. They fell into a routine where Black Ivy would wait on the men and younger women while Howard waited on the rest of the women and older men. Louie and Zoe (the college girl) took over in the middle of the afternoon and followed the same routine. Black Ivy stayed to see how things went and to putter around in the gift shop. Nobody came in the shop but a few people bought Louie's traveling DVDs at the pumps.

All in all, Elly thought it was a good week; Black Ivy's off and running and Ray impressed the silly Willows.

HOLY HANDOUTS

"WHAT DID JESUS DO FOR A LIVING?" Asked one of the kids at church. Ray's still responding to the question and answer cards at Monday Night Church and this one caught him by surprise. He didn't have to answer it (that's why he uses cards instead of live questions from the floor) but he hadn't heard this before and thought it would be an interesting matter to consider. It was from a boy whose parents have been after him to do better at school so that he can get a good education that will lead to a good job so that he'll be able to support himself and not be a bum. He wanted to know how Jesus paid for *his* food and clothing, and where did he sleep? Did he rent a room and, if he did, how did he get the money to pay for it? Ray talked about kindness, hospitality, sharing and so forth and how much Jesus did for others, but afterwards, as they were shaking hands with people on their way out, the boy comes up, he was about eleven, and says: "So, you're basically saying he depended on handouts, like a hobo?" Ray explained the arrangement as best he could; the parents apologized and Elly heard them scolding the kid on their way to their car. It was an awkward moment. Later, Ray told her that it's a tricky area and reminded her that they (the Ollie Khans) are not Christians (actually, up until their meeting with the Willows where Ray explained the charter, Elly assumed they were). He said Ollie and Orchard set up the church as a completely independent, non-denominational and non-affiliated organization. But, Ray added that you have to accommodate Christianity because it's such an integral part of our culture. He says it's difficult to avoid endorsing people's beliefs without offending them in the process.

On the brighter side, Black Ivy's still in business and seems to be doing okay. She and her crew all look sharp in their checkered hats and red bow ties. She's also interviewing for a third worker, since Louie will have to get back to his own business pretty soon. Her revenue has been steady and is gradually increasing. She has the gas priced about ten cents higher than the other stations in the area (to pay for Howard and Zoe), but she says it doesn't seem to be causing customers to stay away; at least business is steady enough and she hasn't heard any complaints. She thinks that since gas is so expensive already, ten cents more a gallon doesn't make much difference. One of her bigger customers are mothers with children, especially with babies in car seats. They thought the single grade of gas would be a problem, but it hasn't been. Most of the customers understand the arrangement (Black Ivy's got a sign explaining it), for the others, if they say: "...regular please," they get the *89 octane*. If they say: "high test," Black Ivy and her crew say: "*89 octane*'s the highest we've got; okay?" And they always say: "Okay," or "Sure."

Louie's displaying one of his cars in the garage bay (an old Lincoln), and his DVDs (the ones he records from the hood of his car as he travels from place to place) are selling pretty well too, but the gift shop (with Bog's knickknacks) has been a bust (nobody parks their car and gets out). Black Ivy's trying to think of another use for the space. Perhaps it could be a hospitality room for traveling preachers with no money.

HAPPY NEW YEAR YOURSELF

IT'S TIME TO THINK ABOUT RESOLUTIONS AGAIN. Elly does this every year but it never works then she feels bad for failing. First, it's like admitting you've got some bad behavior or character flaw to fix. What you're attempting is to make your self start or stop doing something that you already know you should or shouldn't be doing but for some reason, or lack of will, you can't or won't change. Secondly, and whatever the problem is, the root cause of it is probably deeper than you want to admit and is likely beyond the power of any midnight promise to yourself to fix. Black Ivy seems to feel somewhat the same way, at least she's making no resolutions. Says her life is going fine; "... no need to mess with it and I'm not confessing to any faults." Besides, she says she's already got enough to worry about, trying to make the gas station business a success.

Elly asked Bog if he was doing anything. He also says no. Says he doesn't make resolutions on New Years because it's not that important of a date to him. Instead, he says he makes *birthday resolutions*, and claims they work much better since the date is much more meaningful. So she asked him if he had his next birthday's resolution ready to go. He says he's still working on it but it'll be along the lines of being *less* nice. Not that he'll be mean, just "grumpy and disagreeable." He says being pleasant and helpful can be a big liability, causing you a lot of grief and loss of respect, whereas people leave the bullies and bastards alone. So he thinks being a stinker is a much safer attitude. Elly doesn't buy it and thinks he must be having some trouble at work. She knows trouble with the boss or coworkers can make you want to change your personality.

Louie wants to change his girlfriends' personalities. They're big into physical fitness and they've been ganging up on him and nagging him to build up his muscles and put on some weight (like most Asians and many Frenchmen, he's thin as a rail). Ruby was going to resolve to lose ten pounds, but has since changed her mind and has decided to keep the extra weight as a "reserve energy source" in case she gets sick. But she wants Elly to make one: "... to quit smoking those stinking cigars!" Elly said "maybe next year." It's a small vice and she doesn't smoke that many anyway. And if it weren't for her, Ray would have to smoke alone.

She asked Ray if he had any improvements in mind. He said no, but he does plan to do more drawing and maybe even some painting next year. Ruby thinks he could even make a little money at it. He says it's very satisfying to create something, especially something that might last a while. Martha (the hollow woman) told him (Elly can't picture her talking) that artwork has endurance because people seldom discard it, so it's a good way to be remembered. Martha also advised him to move beyond portraits and to show people living, that is doing something (Elly recalled that's sort of what the door-to-door artist that came to the Inn last summer did). Perhaps she's right, Elly thought she'd like to try a little sculpting, seems like it'd be fun. She could make little people and show them doing something. Maybe that'll be her resolution: to be a famous cigar smoking sculptress. At least it's not admitting to any character flaws.

FUGITIVES ON THE LOOSE

BOOLIE'S BACK. Elly was helping Black Ivy clean out the gift shop at the gas station, which she's converting to a small kitchen for making coffee to sell to the gas customers while they're waiting for their tanks to fill (kind of a coffee carhop affair). As she was looking outside watching Howard and Zoe running the pumps, he pulled up in a small delivery truck. She ducked behind the edge of the window and kept an eye on him. He got his gas and left. Zoe later said that he was there buying gas last week too; paid with a company credit card.

Louie says people often stick with the same gas station (once they find one they're comfortable with) so, most likely, he'll be back. Black Ivy lit up and said: "Great! We can grab the bastard!" She and Elly went to the post office to see if they could find his wanted poster (they don't have them on display anymore but you can ask for them at the counter). They finally found it (it was a bad picture): he's wanted for assault and battery with a $2,000 reward for information leading to his arrest. Black Ivy says they can get him when he comes to the station again. She also said it's too bad they don't have the "Dead or Alive" option anymore

Instead, she's working with Louie and Bog to come up with a safe and quick way to snag him. They're focusing on disabling the truck and blocking his doors (while he's parked at the pumps) trapping him inside the vehicle and holding him there until the police arrive. Black Ivy's all excited about nailing him but it sounded like trouble to Elly. At least Black Ivy doesn't have anything lethal in mind.

At the same time, the police were almost after Ray. His illegal motor home setup has been discovered by the town. He received an eviction order from the Building Inspector (he's the guy who also enforces the zoning bylaws) to vacate immediately. So Ray's homeless again and staying at the Inn temporarily. He wanted to build another illegal residence out of an old van that Louie has in back of his garage, but they've talked him out of it. Ruby still wants him to move in and live at the Inn, but he's still against it. Elly's been wanting to move out herself, she's very happy at the Inn but she feel like she's mooching off of Ruby. So they've agreed to look for an apartment nearby to rent together. Elly would like her and Ray to buy a little place (between the two of them, they could probably afford a modest mortgage) but Ray says he couldn't bear to be tied down that tightly. Together, they can handle about $900 a month, so they should be able to find some sort of apartment, but it has to be within walking distance of the church and the Inn, since they don't have a car. (They don't want to borrow Ruby's any more than they already do.) Louie, on the other hand, wants them to buy a fairly reliable old Volkswagen Jetta he has for just his cost: $2000. Ray, again, said no thanks. He seems to have an aversion to owning much of anything, and he seems to be avoiding putting down any roots. Elly told Black Ivy that she's always afraid that he'll grab his bag and disappear at any moment. There's nothing holding him here. Ruby says if their entrapment scheme works for Boolie, perhaps they could try it on Ray.

NO CIGARS

NO SIGN OF BOOLIE YET, but Black Ivy and her gang are ready and expect him at any moment. It'll be a three person operation. First, there'll be three long nylon cargo straps (the adjustable kind with big hooks on each end) stretched crosswise on the ground, under the center of where the truck will be parked. When Boolie stops, Black Ivy will distract him while Howard or Zoe (depending who's on duty) will slide a floor jack under the back and lift the rear axel off the ground (so he can't drive away). At the same time, Black Ivy will pick up the straps (one at a time from the driver's side) and throw them over the roof to the passenger side where Louie will catch them, hook the ends together and pull them tight, while Howard or Zoe is inside calling the police. The key feature is speed, it all has to be done before Boolie can think to react. They've practiced on Orchard's old pickup (now the Church truck) and can do it in under seven seconds.

Meanwhile, speed is also the key to Black Ivy's car side coffee business. She's up and running and, just like the gas, the strategy is simplicity. There are no choices to slow things down, you get one size (medium), no de-caf, and cream and sugar (in little packets) whether you ask for it or not. It's some kind of high-class Vermont coffee that seems to be fairly popular.

The thought was, that people would want to get a coffee while waiting for their fill-up, and that *has* been the case; but the opposite is also true: where some people are driving in just for the coffee, and some getting their tanks topped off while they're at it. Kind of a dual reciprocating business. Black Ivy's pretty happy with it and Bog wants her to add donuts to the mix, but she says no. Ray suggested cigars; says they're very popular now. Again, Black Ivy said no. Cigars just remind her of Clinton's shameful escapades that she'd rather forget. (Elly realized she'll have to avoid smoking in front of her.)

Ruby can't forget the Clintons either and was furious when Hillary ran for for President and is worried that she'll try agin. Even if she ever won a Primary, Bog says it's unlikely that she could get elected. He says that her base is too limited. Although most any Democrat can carry the Northern industrial states, they need to find a way to win at least some of the South, and it probably didn't sit well with them when Hillary abandoned Arkansas to pick up New York's Democrat friendly Senate seat.

That made Ruby feel a little better until Ray said he wasn't so sure. Noting that the Republican era is over, he says it'll be a while before another gets elected. Ruby says not if a better Republican like that nice Mitt Romney down in Massachusetts runs again. Ray says that could be trouble. If Romney got the next nomination, his religion would get a lot of attention and concerns are bound to come up; not only the usual racial and polygamy problems, but also other Mormon peculiarities like magic seeing stones, treasure hunting, Masonic under garments and their suspect *Book of Mormon* origins. Ruby says religion shouldn't matter, Ray says these days, religion matters a lot and if voters think the religion's wacky, they'll think Romney's wacky and that could be Hillary's eventual ticket back to the White House. Ruby says someone should strap Ray into a truck and drag *him* away.

HAULED OFF

THE POLICE HAVE BOOLIE. As Louie predicted, he returned for another fill-up. Black Ivy and her crew were ready. When they saw him come in and stop, straddling the straps (three of them laid out crosswise on the parking platform), Black Ivy came out of the office with a free cup of hot coffee (without the lid). Once the coffee was in Boolie's surprised hands, Louie strolled out and stood by the passenger side of the truck as Zoe, from behind, slid the floor jack (that was waiting beside the pump) under the rear differential and had the wheels off the ground in five pumps of the handle. At the same time, Black Ivy picked up one of the straps and tossed it over the cab to Louie while Boolie watched.

Louie already had the other end of the strap in his hand and hooked them together and cinched them snug. Boolie sat up straight, twisted his head from left to right several times, then started his engine. Black Ivy had already thrown the second strap and was throwing the third. Louie fastened them as Zoe ran inside and called the police. Boolie tried to drive off. When he realized his wheels were spinning in the air, he hollered at Louie and Black Ivy to let him down and threw himself against the door trying to force it open, but the straps held tight. He then thrashed from left to right, trying to rock the truck off of the jack but only managed to splash coffee everywhere. Then, to everyone's horror, he threw out the remains of the coffee and started to cut the straps! They hadn't planned on that. He frantically work on the center strap with a small tool (they think it was nail clippers). His elbow was flying as he continued to holler and rev his engine. He eventually cut through one and was working on the second when the police pulled in.

"You're only suppose to *provide information* about the fugitives, not *apprehend* them!" barked the first angry officer.

Black Ivy didn't flinch and, with her dark Egyptian eyes sharpened, says: "Here's your *information*: This fugitive (she handed them a copy of the wanted poster) is in his truck waiting for you to take him away!" With scowling frowns and guns drawn, they unstrapped the truck, got Boolie out, handcuffed him and escorted the fugitive to the back of their cruiser. On the way, Boolie turned to Black Ivy and thrust his chin toward her and seemed to say: "By Faley you *weel all* die for this!" They made Black Ivy sign something and quietly left. Later, someone came and towed away the pickup. After just a little cleaning up, you'd never know anything had happened and business returned to normal. Black Ivy was thrilled; says her heart was beating a mile a minute. Elly was glad she wasn't there.

Howard was sorry he missed the event but was glad Zoe did such a great job. However, it shook Zoe up quite a bit and said she felt she had to quit, so now Black Ivy's looking for *two* people to hire. Later, she went to the Post Office to see if there are any other local fugitives available. Bog's worried about the whole business. He says Boolie will eventually get out of jail and he might be looking for a little retaliation. Black Ivy said: "Let him try." But later confided to Elly that she's decided to get a gun.

Elly was a little shook up herself, at least Ray thinks so. He's decided that they should go on a trip for a few months. He doesn't want her to worry about where but says she'll need a passport.

She resigned from the Blues Club and is showing Louie how to run the radio station. So her future's unclear but she feels it should be okay. She thinks she'd like to go to Brazil; perhaps she can trade her knife for some nuts.

- End -

Thanks to:

AJ
B. Harrie
The Hollands
Jim & Betty
Len
Oz & Libby
Princess

www.ingramcontent.com/pod-product-compliance
Lightning Source LLC
Chambersburg PA
CBHW031349040426
42444CB00005B/238